Musical Discourse

MUSICAL DISCOURSE

From The New York Times

By

RICHARD ALDRICH

Essay Index Reprint Series

BOOKS FOR LIBRARIES PRESS, INC.
FREEPORT, NEW YORK

First Published 1928
Reprinted 1967

LIBRARY OF CONGRESS CATALOG CARD NUMBER:
67-28740

PRINTED IN THE UNITED STATES OF AMERICA

I am deeply indebted to Adolph S. Ochs, Esq., publisher of "The New York Times," for permission to use in this book matter that has appeared in that journal; and to A. H. Fox Strangways, Esq., editor of "Music and Letters," for permission to use matter published in his periodical.

RICHARD ALDRICH

Contents

Musical Discourse

PROGRAMME MUSIC

THE "modernists" announce several changes that they are intending to introduce into musical art. Some of them will have naught to do any more with emotion or, indeed, with "expression" of any sort. By others "programme music" is no longer to be tolerated; it is dead. Both these innovations are revolutionary. From its earliest days music has meant emotion, of one kind and degree or another. Also there has been an effort, more or less groping and, till its systematization in recent years, more or less tentative, to make music express what is now called a "programme"; to make it represent something outside of itself—what the romantic musicians of the last century were pleased to call the "poetic idea." As Michel Brenet remarks in a study of the origin of descriptive music, the first musician who anticipated the exclamation of Correggio, "Anch' io sono pittore!" is lost in the crowd of his unnamed colleagues of the Middle Ages. Yet the expression of something outside of itself seems really alien to the nature of music. Music calls up and establishes moods; it suggests things that are not to be expressed in words. It embodies emotions, passions, longings, aspirations, inward states of mind. It touches the deeper things, also the lighter things of life and human experience. But it does so in its own way. It speaks its own language; and this is not the language of description or narrative or anecdote —not even the language of poetry. But this effort at exterior expression that has persisted so long in the aims and ideas of musicians has presumably some basis in the art or in its reaction upon listeners.

There was much talk in the France of the earlier eighteenth century about "truth" and the "imitation of nature" in music. Essayists and critics universally agreed that the imitation of nature was the sole aim and object of music. Musicians, especially composers, were somewhat less certain of it; but there were innumerable pieces in the French literature of the harpsichord and violin in the first half of the eighteenth century wherein composers assiduously pursued the imitative path laid down for them. Those who imitated defectively, or who made no attempt at imitation were severely criticised. Instrumental music offered something of a problem to the doctrine of the imitation of nature, so it was generally set down as something inferior. How was it possible to enjoy music that in itself represented nothing? The words of Fontenelle have become famous: "Sonate, que me veux tu?" In the latter half of the century the ground was shifted; and Rousseau could write: "Music does not express things directly, but evokes in the mind the same sentiments that are felt in seeing them." Criticism gradually came around to a belief that "states of the soul" rather than natural objects were the things suitable for music to deal with. It was, in this matter, belated; behind the dilettanti, and the musicians themselves. But by the later years of the century the "imitation of nature" was little more heard of. More systematic and determined efforts at musical delineation were to come in the following century.

The aesthetician will tell us that music and architecture are the two arts that by nature are self-determined; that express themselves, that function within their own limits. The aestheticians, however, seem to have got only a very short way in music. We "hear great argument about it and about"; but ever more come out by that same door wherein we went. Perhaps their dictum about it is not necessarily final. Musicians have been struggling against it ever since there have been musicians.

Programme music has always involved more or less laborious effort, the resort to artifice, the adoption of conventions, the agreement upon a barren symbolism of one kind or another. Music expresses "musicality"; it is incommensurable with ideas outside of music, ideas of another category. What it may be taken to express more than itself is something attributed to it by some convention, some association, either natural or incongruous; or by some kind of hieroglyphic or symbol not essentially part of the music itself.

A wise professor of that modern branch of study, "appreciation of music," was asked by an earnest pupil what he supposed Beethoven "meant" by the first theme of the "Eroica" symphony. There is the title, "Heroic"; there is the statement of the composer's intention to commemorate a great man; there is the fact that Napoleon Bonaparte's name appeared on the manuscript and was afterwards roughly removed by Beethoven in a rage, at the news of his hero's assumption of the imperial title. There is the funeral march, obviously showing that the hero died and was worthy of great music. There are the other movements, with a less evident intention. But the first movement is unlabelled; must not its themes all have some "meaning" cognate with the conception of a great hero? The wise professor answered that he knew just what Beethoven meant by the first theme; and going to the pianoforte he played:

etc.

with the comment, "That is what he meant." A truer answer never was given. Beethoven's ideas were musical ideas and what he wrote expressed what he meant. When composers have tried upon occasion to make their music "mean something" besides music, it has been done only by dint of explanation, suggestion, hint, or convention, conveyed to the listener's mind by some other medium than the music, which he must gain before he begins to listen. If he attempt to offer his own explanation without being so forewarned, he is very likely to join the ranks of those who have ludicrously failed.

The ranks of those who have so failed in considering the "Eroica" symphony are numerous. Oulibicheff saw in the first movement Napoleon's Egyptian campaign: the gallop of cavalry, bayonet charges by the Old Guard. In the working-out section he found again Egypt, proved to him conclusively by the episode of "a melody, E minor, oboe and 'cellos of Oriental color." Nobody else, apparently, has ever seen this. Von Lenz perceives in this movement a reference not only to Napoleon but also to all heroes; and, coming down to details, in the long passage of syncopation in the working-out section, counts just the thirty-two dagger thrusts that laid Cæsar low at the base of Pompey's statue. For Marx, the first movement is an idealized, abstract picture of a battle, which he traces in vivid detail. The annotator of the early programmes of the New York Philharmonic Society, in the 'forties of the last century, thought that "the simple subject, keeping its uninterrupted way through harmonies that at times seem in almost chaotic confusion, is a grand idea of Napoleon's determination of character." And this last kind of generality is as far as the more sophisticated exegetes of recent years, as well as some earlier ones, are willing to go. Grove finds in the work "a portrait—we may believe, a favorable portrait— of Napoleon"; it "should be listened to in that sense." To Kretzschmar it is not the picture of a battle but of a heroic nature. Bekker leaves the programme, and philosophizes, *more Teutonico*, of the movement as " a rebirth of form out of the spirit of poesy." Heuss finds political rather than warlike ideas in the movement. Berlioz declares that there is no question of battles or triumphal marches here, but "thoughts, serious and profound, melancholy memories, ceremonies imposing by their grandeur and sadness, in a word, the funeral oration over a hero"; and especially in the allegro, "the voice of despair and then of rage, and finally, in softer phrases, all that memory can beget of tender grief, in the soul."

[8]

Programme Music

Wagner, as we are fain to think, arrives nearest the truth as he ends his paean on the symphony thus: "Only in the master's tone speech was the unspeakable to be proclaimed—the thing that words here could but darkly hint at." *

II

The programme composer may have the clearest intentions as to what he is going to convey in his music. But suppose he changes his mind about the significance of his music, without changing the music? Is the comprehending listener expected to be comprehending enough to perceive it without instructions? This thing happened in the case of one of the most distinguished landmarks of programme music, Berlioz's "Symphonie Fantastique." Berlioz, in 1829, was greatly smitten with the charms of Harriet Smithson, an unmusical English actress who suddenly captured the hearts of the Parisian public as a member of Charles Kemble's visiting company. Berlioz dreamt of capturing her heart through the power of a grand composition, which he would conduct in London, and by which he would win his triumph by her side. This was to be the "Symphonie Fantastique." He got on slowly with its composi-

* Ellis's translation.

tion. But at the end of two years of waiting and unremitting anguish, he experienced a very sudden cure; unpleasant stories about Miss Smithson reached him; a new divinity captured his heart. The Smithson, however, was by no means forgotten. That very work, intended once for her glorification, should now be turned into an engine for her destruction, punishing her wicked indifference. The "Symphonie Fantastique" should be his revenge. He returned to work on it with savage joy and it was finished. He meant to have it performed in Paris in May, 1830. There were to be printed notes distributed among the audience, so that everybody should understand his cruel allegory. Miss Smithson was to be enticed to the performance, to be recognized by the audience. His triumph and his revenge were to make him famous. This precious scheme fell through; there was no performance and Berlioz walked the streets in debt for the copying of the parts. In the following December he secured a performance of three movements of the symphony. Miss Smithson had returned to Paris in the meantime and had met with reverses; but she cut her quondam admirer dead the first time she saw him, and he determined to go on with the vengeance. The lady escaped it again. The symphony had another performance, but she went somewhere else that evening and never heard of what was impending. At last a complete performance took place, in 1832. Miss Smithson, now completely "down and out" as an actress, was present, at last, in a box; and the public turned a curious gaze upon her. But the composer had in the meantime been jilted by his newer love and had changed his mind again about Miss Smithson and the purposes of the "Symphonie Fantastique." It was once more a pledge of his adoration. She accepted it as a tribute, though she knew little of what it was all about. They were married and lived unhappily, not forever after, but until they separated and Berlioz went off with another lady.

Among the changes that were made in the "meaning" of the symphony was that by which all its movements, instead of only the last two (the "March to the Scaffold" and the "Witches' Sabbath"), were supposed to be the dream of an opium-eating student. Originally the rest were realities; the student dreams that he kills his mistress and is punished for it. It doesn't seem to make much difference so far as the listener is concerned whether he dreams it or really does it. The lady who, in the last movement is represented as a "courtesan," in Berlioz's own word, by the distortion and grimacing transmogrification of the "idée fixe," is of course no longer Harriet

Smithson, as she was in the beginning. Some of the vivid touches in Berlioz's original explanation of the symphony—his "prospectus," as Schumann called it—were naturally cut out in the notes provided for the performance that was finally in Miss Smithson's honor. But the music remained the same. It may also be noted that the persistent theme, the "idée fixe," that symbolizes the lady herself, was transferred by Berlioz from his (unsuccessful) Roman prize cantata, "Hermione." But what matter? It did for the Hermione of his imagination; it would do for the Harriet Smithson of his only too actual passion. It is further to be said that the "March to the Scaffold" was a transference of a "March of the Guards," containing no allusion to hemp or guillotine, from his opera of "Les Francs Juges," of which only the overture now remains. Into this, at suitable intervals, the "idée fixe" was inserted. The "Witches' Sabbath," also, was an appropriation of certain sketches made before the "Symphonie Fantastique" was ever thought of; into which appropriate distortions of the "idée fixe" were also inserted. Altogether, this remarkable piece of programme music, this starting-point of the great nineteenth century movement for "poetic delineation" in music, presents a queer and somewhat amusing appearance in the light of its history; and suggests that its composer was playing fast and loose with his listeners; and, indeed, with the great idea of poetic delineation itself.

An amusing possibility is suggested by Felix Weingartner in his book, "Akkorde," of a man who went to hear a performance of Strauss's "Ein Heldenleben," but thought he was going to hear the same composer's "Symphonia Domestica," and was disastrously supplied with programme notes for this latter. Here is what happened to him: He hears the swinging opening theme of "The Hero"; calls it "Happy Life together of the Married Couple." When the cackling passages come that hold the critics and opponents of the Hero up to scorn, he hears a "Scolding Child." The long passage for violin solo that stands for "The Hero's Wife" presents itself to the misguided listener as "The Wife's Caprices"—nor would there be any very wide departure here from the original intention. The "Battle Scene" comes on; but its thunderous noise and dissonance scarcely outweigh what in the calculation of a Strauss might perfectly well stand for a dispute between man and wife instead of between nations—the real "Symphonia Domestica" goes quite as far, and its depiction of the marital jar might be the crack of doom on the Judgment Day.

Musical Discourse

Then comes "The Hero in his Works of Peace," a celebrated passage in which Strauss makes many quotations from his own previous compositions, throwing modesty to the winds to make it perfectly clear who the "Hero" really is. This would, of course, be taken for the passage in the "Symphonia Domestica" that represents the husband withdrawing himself from domestic contention into his sanctum for his work in composition. Here he again sets forth many of his own musical works. Then the last section of "Ein Heldenleben," the "Flight from the World," might perfectly well be the "Restoration of Marital Felicity." There is a somewhat different sequence of ideas here from what is supposed to be delineated in the real "Symphonia Domestica"; but there is hardly a thing in it that would not be about as plausible for a supposititious "Symphonia Domestica" as it is for an actual "Heldenleben." And then, it is not unprecedented that a listener gets a little confused in trying to follow closely the printed programme analysis. The misled listener might remain in blissful ignorance of his mistake from the beginning of the piece to the end, finding nothing to puzzle him in his exegesis of the composer's ideas or to disturb admiration of the skill and resource with which he had made music express what he was picturing.

Programme Music

The fact is, as Weingartner goes on to say, that even the most monstrous orchestra, even the most ingenious tonal mixtures, coloring and instrumental effects, are unable to bring us a single step nearer the goal proposed by the extreme programmatic composer—the depiction of things by music as they can be depicted by speech or by painting. So long as it is considered necessary to inform the listener in any way what he ought to hear in the music, it is practically admitted that music itself cannot express it. This, says Weingartner, is a dilemma from which neither ingenious sophisms nor lofty phrases can effect a rescue. The problem is solved only in one of two ways: either by composing music solely for music's sake, or effecting a real union of two arts in the song, the oratorio or the opera.

Strauss, in the heyday of his programmatic frenzy, went so far as to declare that a day would come when a composer could compose the silverware on the table so that the listener could distinguish the spoons from the forks. He told a friend that he need not introduce him to his wife, as he had met her in hearing "Ein Heldenleben," and that when he went to Berlin he would be able to identify her from the long violin solo in that composition. He told Felix Mottl that he was proud of the fact that in "Don

Juan" he had so delineated one of the libertine's victims that everybody must recognize that she had red hair. Even if these statements are not taken *au pied de la lettre*, and a little allowance is made for one rapt by the enthusiasm of successful creation, it is evident that he has long looked upon the mission of music to be solely the exact illustration of an anecdote of greater or less importance.

Strauss has travelled a long road in his convictions concerning programme music since he first started on that road. It would seem as if in his later programmatic works he had really come to believe that everybody ought to know what the music means without an explanatory programme; while earlier in his progress he was not prepared to ask so much. His first production that looks toward the programmatic idea is the symphonic fantasia, "Aus Italien," in which he goes only to the very usual and moderate length of giving a descriptive title to each movement. Over the one called "In the Ruins of Rome" he put the somewhat naïve notice that it is "a fanciful picture of vanished glories; feelings of melancholy and grief, in the brilliant sunlight of the present." His next work, "Macbeth," has the label "Macbeth" affixed to the first theme; and to a later passage the words of Lady Macbeth: "Hie thee hither, that I may pour my spirits in thine ear and chastise with the valor of my tongue." "Don Juan," the next in order of composition (though not bearing the next opus number), has as its explanation extended excerpts from Nicolas Lenau's "Faust." "Death and Transfiguration" has prefixed to the score a long descriptive poem by his friend Alexander Ritter, which, it is stoutly affirmed, was written after the completion of the work and in which, it may be assumed, the composer's friend acted as his poetical mouthpiece in formulating the ideas meant for delineation in the music. Here, for the first time, we come upon a definite statement of definite scenes that the composer wishes his hearers to visualize as the music is played. In "Till Eulenspiegel" Strauss had evidently come to think that his music made things so perfectly plain that no explanations were necessary; for he made his well-known reply to Wüllner's request for a programme, that he could furnish none; "were I to put into words the thoughts which the several incidents suggested to me, they would seldom suffice, and might even give rise to offence." He therefore left to his hearers the "hard nut to crack"; all he would do was to point out two "Eulenspiegel" motives. "Also Sprach Zarathustra" is inscribed on the title-page,

Musical Discourse

"freely after Nietzsche"; and there is on the fly-leaf a quotation of "Zarathustra's Preliminary Discourse," addressed to the sun, from Nietzsche. The several sections of the work have titles drawn from Nietzsche's book. Yet, after there had been criticism of this "attempt to compose a cosmic philosophy" in music, Strauss was moved to come out into print and say, "I did not intend to write philosophical music or portray Nietzsche's great work musically. I meant to convey musically an idea of the development of the human race; from its origin through its various phases of development, religious as well as scientific, up to Nietzsche's idea of the Uebermensch." All of which appears to be a distinction without any very great difference, especially considering the quotations from Nietzsche in the subtitles. When he reached "Don Quixote" Strauss apparently had some uncertainty about disclosing all his intentions. He compromised by saying nothing about them in the orchestral score, but labelling every episode of the pianoforte arrangements carefully and fully. Why he entrusted them to the pianoforte players and withheld them from the orchestral conductors is not made clear. "Ein Heldenleben" originally went the whole length of standing by itself without any explanation. Strauss is quoted as

[18]

saying: "There is no need of a programme. It is enough to know that there is a hero fighting against his enemies." Yet it did not take commentators long to find out that Strauss himself was the hero—the section about the "hero's works" was enough to settle that—and that it is he, his life, and his works that are celebrated, to say nothing of his wife; and that his critics, one mentioned as nearly as possible by name, are lampooned.

It was the same thing with the "Symphonia Domestica" when that was played for the first time anywhere in New York. Dr. Strauss was perfectly willing to explain to an inquiring visitor exactly what it was all about, wrote out the chief themes for him, affixing their significance to each, and was willing that themes and explanations should be published in a newspaper before the performance. But after he had finished telling about the significance of the different sections of the work, detailing all the different episodes of home life that are so sonorously portrayed in it, he suddenly changed his mind. He refused to allow the account to be printed—until after the first performance. "This time," he said, "I wish my music to be listened to purely as music." That one time, he might have said; for what of the unfortunates who should listen to all subsequent performances, when the account was printed and the cat was out of the bag for every programme annotator? There is in the score itself of the "Symphonia Domestica" but a single programmatic indication; a note that reads, in the very beginning, referring to the new-born child, "The Aunts: just like his papa"; "The Uncles: just like his mama." An intimate friend of the composer who was with him in the throes of composition, confided to this writer that the autograph of the score of the "Symphonia Domestica," as it grew under the composer's hands, was completely peppered over with notes and suggestions like this. They seemed to be the material out of which the music was secreted in the composer's mind—almost as if they were, to him, terms convertible at any time into music. The story, perhaps indiscreet, throws an interesting light on Strauss's methods of composition, such light as Beethoven left for subsequent generations in his sketchbooks. These notes and suggestions have all disappeared except the one mentioned—was that left by accident, or by design? It seems an unimportant detail to be singled out for perpetuation. It is as if, having built up his musical edifice by means of an elaborate scaffolding, Strauss took down the scaf-

Programme Music

folding when he was done with it, leaving the results to stand by themselves.

Since the "Symphonia Domestica," Strauss's only orchestral programmatic tone poem has been his "Alpine Symphony," which denotes a return to the simpler kind of descriptions. There is no philosophy here, not even the telling of a tale or the relation of an anecdote. It suggests a succession of scenes that might be witnessed in an ascent and descent of an Alpine peak. It utilizes, with Strauss's surpassing technical skill, a number of devices that have long been the stock-in-trade of programme musicians and are among the most conventional of subjects: the sunrise, the forest, the brook, the waterfall, the Alpine horn, the cowbell, the thunderstorm, the sunset. There are others less conventional: there is an "apparition"; a bad quarter of an hour "lost in the thicket and bush"; the glacier, with glacial dangers; the view from the summit, a "vision," the rising of mists and the hiding of the sun; an elegy, and the descent. It may be said that in this piece Strauss has shown, in respect of his musical material, the preoccupation of his later years with themes that lend themselves to plastic working and various devices and combinations rather than with musical ideas of specifically musical value—of musical pregnancy, beauty, and expressiveness, apparently an almost inevitable tendency where the composer is not chiefly or wholly preoccupied with musical expression for its own sake. The music is simplicity itself in comparison with some of his earlier works. The conventional formulas of programme music by rule of thumb are, however, more constantly in evidence than in almost any other of Strauss's works of the same sort. There is a theme to denote the ascent of the mountain; it may mean that as well as anything else after you are told. By a prodigy of ingenuity the inversion of this theme denotes the descent; and all is made plain to the earnest listener. Sunrise is shown by a descending theme; this seems at first contrary to the rules of the game, until subtle consideration and deep thought show that "the mountain tops are first lit by the sun's rays, which reach deeper and deeper till the valleys are suffused with light." There is a marvellously realistic depiction of cowbells — by perfectly good real cowbells; another realistic depiction of the whistling of the wind in a storm, by the whistling of the wind in a "wind machine" —a musical assistant that Strauss had availed himself of previously in "Don Quixote" and for a similar purpose. And here, for the present, Strauss has rested in the work of making the orchestra tell anecdotes. His more recent efforts have all been in the form of opera and ballet.

Perhaps the perfect flowering of programmatic delineation is presented in a passage of Ottorino Respighi's orchestral piece, "The Pines of Rome." In this the nightingale is introduced, not by any of the vague and more or less impotent conventionalities that have so long served composers in the matter of nightingales, but by a phonographic record of a real bird's real notes, which is turned on at the proper moment in the score. The effect, it must be confessed, is a little weak; but perhaps improvement in the phonographic art, such as Mr. Edison, with an overflowing optimism, has recently promised, will change this and enable all sorts of natural noises to be used to supplement the poor conventionalities of the orchestra. At present, the use of the phonograph suggests the kind of realism that ebullient art students obtain in pictures for their burlesque exhibitions by pasting bits of real substance upon their canvases.

III

After the death of Camille Saint-Saëns a jocose composition of his that he wrote many years ago for private performance was "released," as the newspapers say, and came to a good many public performances in Europe and America. It was his "Carnival of Animals," in which he got off a number of musical jokes of varying quality. It was a condensation of a theme that had for many years occupied composers from time to time, and with more or less seriousness—the representation of animals in music. It is, in fact, one of the oldest and most widespread forms of programme music. It goes back to some of the early days of the art; has been practised with widely varying degrees of crudeness and skill and has evidently exercised a certain fascination upon all ranks of composers, from the highest to the lowest.

Birds are naturally the most frequent temptation to composers zoölogically inclined. Birds are supposed to make music themselves. A few of them do; but not many have a song that is based on musical intervals known to man and used by him. The cuckoo and the thrush are perhaps the best known of such birds. The writer used to hear by his window a thrush that sang exactly the notes in the first clause of the first theme of Brahms's string quartet in B flat, Op. 67; only the rhythm was different. Let him hasten to say that there is no reason to

[24]

believe that Brahms had ever heard such a bird or
had the slightest intention of putting him into his
music. Some attempts have been made to set down
in musical notation, in technical bird books, the
songs of the whole tribe; they have not conspicu-
ously succeeded, and the results are mostly unrecog-
nizable, because birds do not, as a rule, use definite
musical intervals.

But, of course, the composers go at it in a more
imaginative manner and do not often attempt to
recapture exactly in musical notation what is generally incommensurable with such notation. The
cuckoo's is the simplest bird song, the clearest in-
terval, the easiest to catch with accuracy. Composers have been catching it for a long time. One
of the earliest known pieces of artistic music is also
a piece of programme music — the famous and delightful English round, "Sumer is i-cumen in." It
is in six voices — a canon in four parts with two
free parts in the bass. Scholars date it from the
earlier years of the thirteenth century; and it is by
far the most highly developed piece of music artisti-
cally, as well as the most beautiful and appealing
to our ears, that can be referred to anything like
such an early date. In the refrain, "sing cucu," there
is an evident intention to suggest the cuckoo's song,

though it is not done so plainly as later attempts succeeded in doing.

A hundred or a hundred and fifty years later, at the close of the fourteenth and beginning of the fifteenth centuries, there was an outburst of descriptive music from composers of various parts of Europe. Some are inspired by the songs of birds; some by scenes in nature; others attempt to reproduce the sounds of the chase, the market-place, the battlefield. Michel Brenet gives a list of compositions dating before the year 1420 which suggest or describe the singing or the flight of birds and the cries of various animals. Brenet lists twenty such pieces; twelve being Italian, mostly for two voices; and eight being French, for three. Various schemes were adopted by these pioneers to carry out their purposes: sometimes they used syllables imitating the cries of animals; sometimes a melodic line to suggest—at least on paper—a bird's flight; such symbolism was dear to the mediaeval heart; sometimes a melodic line to rival, even if only symbolically, again, the songs of birds, without an attempt to copy them directly. The French musicians use texts in which there are frequent syllables imitative of bird songs. Of course the cuckoo, who so intelligently pronounces his own name, is much the most popular, as he is the easiest to quote. Jean Martini, in the second half of the fifteenth century, made the cuckoo's call the theme of a mass—it occurs in the tenor part of each of the divisions of the Mass, varied only as to the length of the notes, and submitted to the characteristic contrapuntal treatment of the time. One of the most famous as well as one of the earliest bird pieces was Clément Jannequin's "Chant des Oiseaux," though Brenet mentions and quotes passages from two Spanish "cuckoo songs" for four voices that date from before 1496; and a few years later was published in German a "guck guck" song for six voices. Jannequin's piece appeared in 1528. It is for four voices and the composer attempts to reproduce the songs of several different birds: the oriole, the quail, the cuckoo, to a text that is hardly less than Rabelaisian in its heartiness, its grossness, its full-blooded humor; a joyful picture of nature in springtime that became one of the most popular pieces of its day. It was "admired, reprinted, sung, transcribed, for long years after its composer's death," and it still gives pleasure and amusement when enterprising singers have attempted it.

Italian composers of the same period turned their attention to birds; and when the madrigalists appeared in the latter years of the sixteenth centuty with their fancy for descriptive music, they filled their compositions with imitative accounts of birds, as well as of many other things. This got on the nerves of Vincenzo Galilei, father of the astronomer and a zealous musical amateur, to such an extent that in his "Dialogo" (1581) he complains bitterly of the rage for musical depiction that had possessed the composers of his own and the immediately preceding period. As Brenet remarks, a study of these compositions would supply material for a curious lexicon of descriptive vocal composition. Such a vocabulary would contain a mass of stereotyped locutions, such as always grow up from one period to another to form the material of "descriptive music" — there is a modern mass of such locutions, just as there was an ancient one — commonplaces almost mechanically transmitted from one musician to another.

Composers of the sixteenth and seventeenth centuries played with the cuckoo considerably. Girolamo Frescobaldi, who lived from 1583 to 1643, produced a cuckoo piece, which is one of the finest and most ingenious musically of such things, his "Capriccio on the Cuckoo's Call," in which he makes the bird's note take part in a fine and effective con-

Programme Music

trapuntal fabric. There is Johann Caspar Kerll's "Capriccio Kuku"—he lived from 1627 to 1693—which Handel, after his fashion of taking his own wherever he found it, appropriated in one of his organ concertos, without, however, calling attention to the cuckoo call (plain enough, when you once hear it)—or to the name of the original author. In his "borrowings" he never did that. François Couperin, an inveterate programme composer if you believe in all his titles, amused himself sometimes with cuckoos and nightingales; but it is often harder to hear them in the music than to see them in the titles. One of the most familiar cuckoos is that of Claude Daquin, whose little harpsichord piece often appears in concert programmes. There are also less familiar Italian pieces of the same sort for harpsichord, such as Bernardo Pasquini's "Toccata with the Cuckoo Joke," whose title suggests what he thought of the business.

Johann Sebastian Bach, in his younger days, did not disdain the cuckoo and his note, as may be seen in the last movement of his clavier sonata in D, in which he imitates and marks, so that none shall miss it, the call of the cuckoo and the crowing of the cock. It should be said, however, that all editions do not reproduce these inscriptions; and still further, that there is doubt in the minds of some whether the piece is really by Johann Sebastian or not. One of the most distinguished of cuckoos is he who is allowed to utter four calls in the slow movement of Beethoven's "Pastoral" symphony. More modern cuckoo calls are heard in the second act of "Hänsel und Gretel," where the two children are getting lost in the wood; and in the first movement of Mahler's first symphony, in which he celebrates Spring. And there are numerous others. The great thing about the cuckoo in music is that it is absolutely unmistakable. It is, for all practical purposes, just as good as the real article. Here programme music reaches its highest point, makes its greatest triumph. No programme note is necessary. The listener need not be left to listen to the cuckoo's song as "absolute music" first, and then get the explanation afterward. He swallows it all immediately.

The hen and the rooster have a respectable place in programme music also. In early days they were almost as much favored as the cuckoo. There is a rooster's note in the piece by Bach — if it is by Bach — just mentioned. In Bach's " Passion according to St. Matthew," after Peter had thrice denied Christ, the Evangelist relates that the cock crew; and the inflection of his voice in imitation of the crowing note is unmistakable. In the parallel passage in the "Passion according to St. John," however, Bach refrains from this imitation. In the newer music many will remember Saint-Saëns's rooster whose crow at midnight disperses the crew of ghostly dancers in the "Danse Macabre." There is a clavier piece by Rameau, called "La Poule" devoted to the hen, in which he has written in, under the henlike notes, the henlike syllables "co-co-co-co-co-co-co-dai," making the point plain to the meanest intelligence. Not very far removed from the henyard is the squawking of the white peacocks in "Salome," which the panic-stricken Herod offers to Salome, if she will forego her request for John the Baptist's head.

The nightingale is a bird beloved of musicians, though his song is of a complication that permits of hardly more than a conventional representation in music, unless the trouble is taken to make a phonograph record of it, as Respighi did. The "fierce noises of the fiery nightingale" have not generally seemed so fierce to composers as they did to Swinburne. The earlier bird-composers generally gave the nightingale up as an insoluble problem and resorted to purely symbolical methods to represent him. They resorted a good deal to imitative syllables, which is, of course, only a way of dodging the difficulty; or they used certain melodic formulas which became conventional — as melodic formulas of all sorts are very apt to. Later composers became more daring or more ingenious. The little piece for harpsichord by Couperin, called "Le Rossignol en Amour" has some elaborate trilling, which is as near as he undertook to get on the harpsichord to the nightingale. In a footnote he gives a suggestion that his successors have followed only too well. "This nightingale cannot succeed better than on the flute, when it is well played." Thenceforth flutes and nightingales have been almost inseparable in music. Handel, in his "L'Allegro, il Pensieroso ed il Moderato" has a famous number in the soprano air, "Sweet Bird that Shunn'st the Noise of Folly," beloved still by coloratura singers, in which the flute vies with the voice in representing the nightingale's gushes of song. Few, if any, to-day have heard a performance of Handel's opera of "Rinaldo." In that is the air "Augelletti che cantate," with an elaborate accompaniment of two flutes and a flageolet — a "recorder" — warbling the song of the nightingale. It was during a performance of this air, when the opera was given in Handel's London opera house, that a flock of live birds was let loose on the stage, moving Joseph Addison to one of his most amusingly sarcastic and derisive papers in *The Spectator* against the Italian opera.

In his oratorio of "Joshua," Handel has suggested the song of the linnet and thrush by a duet between the violin and flute in the air, "Hark, 't is the Linnet and the Thrush." Rameau also went elaborately into the nightingale's warbling in the air "Rossignols Amoureux," in the opera of "Hyppolite et Aricie," which was long a favorite of florid singers. Felicien David, in his opera of "La Perle du Brésil," celebrates with the most elaborate kind of flutings the song of a mysterious kind of bird called the "mysoli," in the air "Charmant Oiseau," also still beloved of coloratura singers, though the opera itself has long been extinct. There is a song by the Russian composer Alabieff that was once much sung, and much transcribed by purveyors of brilliant pianoforte pieces. And this list could be much enlarged. In fact, song-writers are rarely able to resist the temptation, when the text they are treating mentions the nightingale, to mention it also, even if ever so briefly, in their accompaniment.

The nightingale also gets a look in in Beethoven's "Pastoral" symphony, where, in the "Scene by the Brook" in the slow movement he makes his appearance alongside the cuckoo and the quail.

Musical Discourse

Beethoven's quail, however, has a note different from that of the "bob-white" of this country. In Haydn's "Creation," too, the nightingale "with her soft, enchanting lay" (though it is only the male bird that sings) makes an appearance with suitable accompaniment on the wind instruments, together with the " eagle on mighty pens," "the merry lark," and " the tender dove that, cooing, calls his tender mate " all appropriately figured in the instrumental accompaniment.

Of unspecified birds the literature contains an abundance. Siegfried's bird is the most eloquent and the most beautiful singer of them all, unmatched by any other bird in music. There are the birds with which Nedda sings in the second scene of "Pagliacci." You can hear miscellaneous birds in innumerable pianoforte pieces, from Rameau's "Rappel des Oiseaux" down to the present time: in Liszt's account of " St. Francis Preaching to the Birds"; in Henselt's aerial bird study. You can hear birds in most "Spring" symphonies and overtures; as in the first movement of Mahler's first symphony which he calls "Spring and no End"; or in Goldmark's "Spring" overture; or d'Indy's symphony called "Jour d'Eté sur la Montagne."

Of other and less specifically musical animals the

horse has been the favorite of composers, of course because of the rhythmic qualities of his hoof-beats. Perhaps he has never been more thrillingly represented than in the "Ride of the Valkyries" in Wagner's music drama. Schubert more simply thrills with the horse's onward rush in "The Erlking." Liszt represents the steed of the Ukrainian breed that bore Mazeppa through the symphonic poem of that title. Raff depicts the galloping of the dead lover's horse bearing away Lenore in the symphony so named. Franck has employed a conventional horse motive in his symphonic poem "Le Chasseur Maudit." Brahms, who rarely put concrete things into music, put the galloping horse into the first song of his "Magelone" set. Perhaps the first of all musical horses are those depicted by Monteverdi in his "dramatic interlude" entitled "Il Combattimento di Tancredi e Clorinda," in 1642.

Saint-Saëns has a jackass in his "Carneval"; though perhaps it is not so stridently vocal as Mendelssohn's in the overture to "A Midsummer Night's Dream," there resonantly represented by the bassoon in the transmogrification of Bully Bottom. A little lower in the scale of animal creation comes the sheep; and a good deal lower than anything yet mentioned in musical zoölogy is Strauss's representation of the flock of sheep in "Don Quixote." Still lower down are the frogs that hop, the flies that buzz, in Handel's "Israel in Egypt," when he describes the plagues of Egypt. Wagner composed a toad in "Das Rheingold" when Alberich "shows off" to Wotan and Loge by taking that shape, and gets into trouble thereby. And he takes the shape of a huge serpent, as Fafner afterwards took that of a dragon, and the same sort of music represents them both. Bees have their place in music, as in Couperin's clavier piece, "Les Abeilles," and in the violin piece of the same name by Franz Schubert (not the great one). Couperin also treats of the fly in "Le Moucheron"; and one of the Strausses of the dragon-fly, which zigzags through an ingenious dance piece. Butterflies appear in Couperin, again, and in Grieg's little pianoforte piece, both called "Les Papillons."

Musical accounts of the chase were scarcely less popular in the middle ages than descriptions of animals. Perhaps the earliest of them was a piece for three voices by one Ghirardello de Florentia, who died at a date unknown, but before 1400. Jannequin, of course, could not keep his hands off this subject, and his piece, "La Chasse," is another lively attempt at realistic description of a sport which easily lent itself to such attempts. His hunting piece was published about 1528 and was the forerunner of numerous others in France and elsewhere, that have extended their lineage down to modern times. The English virginal composers gave some attention to the possibilities of the hunt; the best known of such hunting pieces is Dr. John Bull's "The King's Hunt," as it is called in the Fitzwilliam Virginal Book, elsewhere "The King's Hunting Jigg," though there is nothing of the jig about it.

The composition of Jannequin's that surpassed all his others in popularity was his "Battle of Marignan." As Thayer remarks in his observations on Beethoven's "Battle of Vittoria," few indeed were the great battles of Europe that were not fought over again by orchestras, bands, and all sorts of instruments — even down to an account of the battle of Jena for two flutes, unaccompanied. Jannequin set this fashion; and he himself followed up his first battle with other French victories — battle composers always composed, as battle painters always painted, victories — all, it may be hoped, suitably differentiated so that each conflict may be properly identified. The real battle of Marignan, between the French under Francis I and the Swiss, took place in 1515. Jannequin's piece followed it by some

years; it was very popular and many times reprinted.
It is for four voices, and is full of spirited passages
descriptive of the fighting, in which the composer
leans a good deal upon the text, full of long strings
of imitative, "made up" words, battle-cries, imi-
tations of trumpet calls and other useful material.
It has in recent years been performed for an admiring posterity and has been found to be a really vital
and "amusing" piece. It was transcribed for instruments: for the lute, upon which it could hardly have
been as effective as the battle of Jena for two flutes;
for various combinations of instruments, and for
the organ. Jannequin's battle was naturally the
starting-point for numerous other battles of the
same and subsequent periods. An improvement introduced in some of these was to identify the different troops by their language: the French, Italians,
Spaniards, and Germans sang and shouted in their
own tongues. Jannequin himself introduced still
further improvement in his later "Battle of Metz"
by adding parts for drums and trumpets. It is re-
grettable to notice that in some of his later editions,
when the conflict at Marignan had begun to fade a
little from the memories of men, Jannequin introduced modifications into the text of the "Battle of
Marignan" intended to bring it up to date, make

it apply to another more recent battle, and to celebrate the prowess of a later king — Henri II instead of Francis I. This seems like playing fast and loose with fundamental ideas of programme music.

Another sixteenth century battle piece is by William Byrd, for the virginal, one of the least warlike of instruments, contained in "Lady Nevell's Virginal Book," compiled in 1595. This is not one of the great Elizabethan composer's most successful efforts; it has all the primitive conventionalities of musical battles and none of the pregnant qualities of Byrd's musical style. There are, as in duty bound, "The Marche before the Battell," "The Battell," "The Marche of the Footemen," "The Marche of the Horsmen," "The Trumpetts," "The Irishe Marche," "The Bagpipe and the Drone," "The Flute and the Droome," "The Marche to the Fighte," "The Retreat," and "A Galliarde for the Victorie." A version of the same piece contained in "Elizbeth Rogers's Virginal Book" contributes further "The Buriing of the Dead"; another version in manuscript has "The Morris" and "Ye Souldiers Dance."

"Battle pieces" have made their appearance down to the present time. The most distinguished of them is signed with the great name of Beethoven

Musical Discourse

—"Wellington's Victory; or the Battle of Vittoria." The battle was fought in 1813, and Beethoven was promptly on its heels with his piece, in the same year. It is a year of his life that is barren of great works; and this piece for orchestra does not adorn it. But he seems to have thought pretty well, himself, of "The Battle of Vittoria"; its first performance in Vienna was considered a notable event. The English troops are unmistakably earmarked in it by "Rule, Britannia," as the French are by "Malbrouk s'en va-t'en Guerre." There is the battle, consisting largely of scale passages, and a "symphony of victory," embodying jubilantly "God Save the King," and finally a fugue on it. Beethoven prefaced the piece with a long series of directions for performance. There should be two brass bands, besides the usual orchestra. The two bass drums that represent the cannon fire should be the largest obtainable, and they must be placed in the distance, one on each side, and out of sight. Watchmen's rattles represent the musketry fire, and these must be similarly disposed, as well as the trumpets and snare drums which represent the approach of the two armies. This piece of programme music came five years later in Beethoven's life, it may be observed, than the "Pastoral Symphony," which he

composed with very different ideals in view—
"rather the expression of feeling than actual representation of facts."

Perhaps the most important orchestral battle that has been fought since Beethoven's has been the one in which Strauss's hero is engaged, in "Ein Heldenleben." The art and science of war had made great progress in a century, as is vividly set forth in the discordant sounds of this battle, so much more terrifying than Beethoven's.

Another subject that became popular in descriptive music was the street cries of the towns. A century before Jannequin one Zacharias of Florence had undertaken to represent in choral song the noisy confusion of the bargaining at a street fair; and a hundred years before that, even, the historians find in a famous manuscript (that of Montpellier) the attempt of an unknown composer to base a motet for three voices on a street peddler's cry, "Fresh strawberries, fresh mulberries!" Pierre Aubry, the French musical historian, calls it "the earliest attempt at aesthetic realism in musical history." From the thirteenth century to the twentieth such attempts have persisted, as they can testify who have heard the scene of the street cries in Charpentier's "Louise."

Musical Discourse

Certain composers have hit upon the idea of making paintings the subject of musical illustration, or re-illustration of their subjects. It gets a little involved. The picture itself represents something; then the music makes a dimmer representation of that. Liszt's "Battle of the Huns" is a repainting of Kaulbach's painting in the Pinakothek at Munich. Not everybody has been to the Pinakothek at Munich, or knows what Kaulbach's picture looks like. So they have a double handicap in listening to the symphonic poem. Sergei Rachmaninoff wrote one of his most successful orchestral pieces about Arnold Böcklin's "Isle of the Dead." It is successful as music in spite of, rather than because of, its subject. Hans Huber some years ago wrote a symphony, now pretty well forgotten, about other pictures of Böcklin's, but thought better of it and left the pictorial label only upon the last movement, as avowedly "illustrating" — strange collocation of terms — pictures; but the pictures are unnamed. When a composer insists upon his listeners having knowledge and appreciation of pictures that may be scattered through the galleries of Europe, public and private, as a prerequisite to understanding his music, he is putting a considerable strain upon them. But when he is illustrating pictures "unnamed," he is indulging in a very private sort of amusement. He had better keep silent about the pictures.

There should be mention of another programmatic attempt of William Byrd, one more successful than his battle piece, "The Bells," in the Fitzwilliam Virginal Book; a singularly ingenious representation of the "changes" rung upon a peal of bells in an English church tower, in which the virginal is made to suggest clangorous timbres far beyond its actual possessions.

Composers have taken the phenomena of nature as something they were entitled to work into the fabric of music. The most elemental of them all Haydn wrestled with in the prelude to his "Creation," a piece that now seems by no means chaotic, where chaos is depicted, and then its transformation into the cosmos. The sea as a promising subject for musical description and delineation has by no means been overlooked by composers; but like mountain landscape, the vision of the sea has appealed mostly to the modern intelligence. Rubinstein's "Ocean" symphony, in which he at first resisted the temptation to write a "storm" piece, but finally yielded in one of the three movements that he added to the four of which the work originally

consisted; Rimsky Korsakoff's "Scheherazade" with
its suggestion of the sea sailed by Sindbad; his
"Sadko"; Tchaikovsky's "Tempest," one of many
attempts to carry Shakespeare over into music; Debussy's poetical conception in "La Mer" are what
most easily occur to the memory. There are storms
not only at sea but also on land. One of the earliest
is John Mundy's virginal piece dating from the
early seventeenth century, the "fantasia" depicting "faire wether," "lightning," " thunder," "calme
wether" and "a faire day"—but not depicting any
of it very vividly to modern senses. There is the
classical model of a storm, Beethoven's in the "Pastoral" symphony; and there is the brief disturb-
ance at the end of "Das Rheingold" and the more
ominous one in the prelude to "Die Walküre."

IV

The convinced champions of programme music are
not content to take the composers at their word
and to be satisfied with avowed programme music.
A programme must lurk in every composition that
shows itself to be of any importance and that makes
any effect, whether the composer knew it or not—
at any rate whether he confessed it or not. There was
the late Professor Frederick Niecks, who published

a very thick volume on the subject of programme music. Its thickness was attained by including in its scope almost every composition of importance in the literature of music. It is a veritable bed of Procrustes, upon which each composer is laid and made to suffer. Professor Niecks declares that the definition of programme music should embrace not only the " outward and inward," the general and the particular, not only "music with the programme merely indicated by a title," but also—and here is where we all become M. Jourdain and find we have been listening to this kind of prose all our lives without knowing it—"music the title of which is unrevealed." For, we are told, "the absence of programme and title does not prove the music to be absolute." This ardent advocate even asks, " Is there such a thing as absolute music?" "Are there composers uninfluenced by programme music and averse to it in practice?" To this astonishing question Professor Niecks answers that there are not, either such music or such a composer,—meaning good music, music that we care to hear and really enjoy, music that affects the mind and heart and does not consist merely of unmeaning combinations of sounds. Nothing could be simpler; and nothing could more completely destroy the real meaning of the term "programme music" or invalidate the distinctions which the real programme musicians have been laboring to establish. Thus, though all his life Brahms stood for the very opposite of all that is implied by programme music, in his music Niecks is sure that there is "something connected with life — that is, with the composer's experiences, thoughts, and feelings, with his relations to man and nature." Of course there is; and of course there is in any music that is music at all. In another book, generally sane and sensible, by Professor Spalding ("Music an Art and a Language"), Brahms is invited, or forcibly inserted, into the bed of Procrustes thus: The G minor Ballade seems, "from inner evidence," to be a picture of a knight-errant setting out on his adventures, which include a meeting with a maiden. The conclusion is bewildering: "In this piece is seen Brahms's aristocratic distinction in the treatment of programme music"—the idea that it is programme music at all being a purely unwarranted assumption, contrary to all the practices and professions of the unfortunate composer. R. A. Streatfeild points out in his "Modern Music and Musicians" that all modern instrumental music—at least all that is worth listening to—was really written to express what is called "a poetic subject"; that is, it is not mere music for music's sake, but is meant to describe or depict something else that is not music, some programme that the composer had in mind—though he didn't mean to and didn't say so.

Is not the mistake that writers of this school make that they lose sight of the fact that in music resides an emotional and thrilling power of its own; that without undertaking to interpret or illustrate anything or any idea outside of itself, it may yet exert the most moving influence on the listener; may afford the keenest, most poignant aesthetic delight; that in this way it is in the deepest and truest sense "connected with life"; that though it may not reproduce explicitly any experience of the composer or paint in definite outline any of his thoughts and feelings, it yet is truly the outcome of his experience, of his thoughts and feelings, of his "relations with man and nature" expressed in his way, in accordance with his genius, through his medium, music. Is it not a mistake to think that "absolute" music is simply a kind of tonal arabesque; a superior kind of lamp-shade designing or carpet weaving— a mere playing with patterns and colors? Is it not a mistake to miss the conception that a great master's success in following and building up, enlarging and developing "form" in music, as Beethoven followed and built it up, enlarged and developed the sonata form, as in the first movement of the "Eroica" symphony, means the attainment of a peculiarly rare, recondite, and permanent kind of beauty—a kind of beauty incommensurable with any other expression of it?

Bach's harpsichord piece on the departure of his beloved brother is an obvious attempt at programme music. But Albert Schweitzer, one of the most highly considered biographers of Bach since Spitta, elaborates a theory in his book on the master, charging him heavily with programmatic intentions in many of the two hundred church cantatas and the other choral works left by him. We have mentioned how the cock crows in the "Passion according to St. Matthew," when Peter had thrice denied his master, and the heart-breaking musical phrase which signifies that he thereupon "went out and wept bitterly"; and how, in the "Passion according to St. John," the cock does not crow, though Peter's weeping is not less movingly suggested. This is an obvious and unmistakable instance of the sort of thing Schweitzer undertakes to find scattered thickly through the church cantatas, though generally of a more recondite and, it might be said, conventionalized sort. He purports to exhibit many

Programme Music

different tonal formulas used by Bach to illustrate many different kinds of emotional states and appeals, as well as physical happenings and pictorial suggestions. They are classified and listed, illustrated in the book with musical examples. Now, many curious, amazing, and truly wonderful things are to be found by those who will study the great mass of Bach's choral works. Among them, undoubtedly, are occasionally more or less obvious illustrations of concrete images suggested by the text. It is aside from the point to include the music embodying the deeper emotional states which it is part of the essential function of music to embody. The subject is too far-reaching to be pursued here. But to many it will seem that Schweitzer is obsessed by the idea of finding definite formulas repeatedly used for different and definitely classified purposes; that he goes much too far. There are innumerable passages in the cantatas where Schweitzer's formulas are not used, but would have been had Bach had, consciously or even unconsciously, any such disposition toward systematic programmatic expression as he is credited with.

It is a doctrine of the most recent workers in programme music that the art of music has been "improved" so much and its resources so far developed that it can already express almost everything and ultimately will be able to express quite everything that words can, and probably more. But, as a matter of fact, the devices of the literal programme music makers are often so purely conventional and sometimes so purely technical in character that to those not especially instructed in their significance they have no significance whatever. There are resources, imaginative and suggestive, that have long and often been used to conjure up moods of the most general sort and that are effective in doing so. But these are far from being sufficient for the most advanced programmatic composers. Every student of programme compositions is aware of the barren subtleties and ingenuities of a purely "cerebral" sort, the mechanical and conventional methods, to which they resort in their music in order to work out their schemes. Thus it is often the procedure to affix an arbitrary significance to some well-known melody, which is to have that significance whenever it turns up in the picture they are painting. They must see to it that everybody is given the key to it beforehand, or the listener will come upon a closed door. For instance, in Liszt's symphonic poem "The Battle of the Huns" the trombones begin to intone the Catholic hymn " Crux Fidelis," to indicate that the Christian forces are fighting and that they finally gain success. Those who do not know the "Crux Fidelis" must be informed what it is; and, as in and of itself it does not relate to the battle in which Attila was defeated, the significance which the composer has decided to impart to it must also be conveyed to the listener. Having firmly grasped these points in the game, he may now proceed to hear the orchestrá play it.

The further programme music is pushed toward literalness of expression and exposition of detail, the less that expression becomes like music and the more like some traditional sign language, a collection of hieroglyphics, an expert and technical utterance addressed to the intellect, the memory and the reasoning powers, and not to the imagination or the emotions and the specifically musical feelings of the listener. Such devices as the "inversion" of a theme to denote something conceived of as in some way the opposite of its original significance are typical of the method. An inversion of a theme presents that theme with its intervals reversed in direction, up or down, an equal number of degrees in the scale; so that it is, in a manner of speaking, the theme upside down. As a device of contrapuntal music without ulterior meaning it is of hoary antiquity. The programme composers seized upon it as a convenient and useful hieroglyphic. If a given theme is labelled to mean one thing, let its inversion mean the opposite. The listener must first be informed of the original label, and then must be ready to detect the inversion. As a matter of fact, however, the inversion of any theme of considerable extent or complexity is not easily recognizable by the ordinary listener, or even by the well-informed one; it may often escape detection entirely, and may be overlooked by the professional listener who is not specially on his guard.

Other devices less difficult are the augmentation or diminution of themes — their presentation in a slower or a quicker form; the change of their rhythm; the change of their harmony, perhaps by enrichment or simplification or distortion by discords. All these devices are used by composers innocent of programmatic intentions, as means to enhance the richness or variety of their musical utterance; but the point is that, when they are taken up to give some special arbitrary significance in the delineative scheme, as they so often are, that special significance must generally be conveyed by a printed notice or in some other extra-musical way to the listener. In so far his attention is diverted from the music as music and directed to something outside of itself for some purpose which, though it may be styled "poetic," is at any rate unmusical. These devices cannot speak for themselves in the course of the performance because inherently and essentially they have no such meaning as the composer wishes to attribute to them.

It is an old joke that the programme musician should be asked to compose a symphonic poem describing how an Englishman took a trip to the Continent, changed his religion, and lost his umbrella. The implication was that it could not be done in music. But it would be perfectly possible in the kind of conventional sign language used in the most advanced programme music. Begin with a well-defined English tune and a quotation from "Pinafore," the melody of "He is an Englishman," thus establishing the residence and nationality of the subject, so that it should be clear to the meanest intelligence. The sea has often enough been represented in music; there are excellent models which could be followed or improved upon—a short transition passage, rough or smooth as might be preferred, could indicate the crossing of the Channel. Landing in France plainly calls for a representation of smiling landscape—also an old musical device, in which the more imaginative or poetic suggestiveness of music could be called on — and a determination of French local color by a French tune. Change of religion: Let the hero's original Anglicanism be denoted by some sound selection from the Hymnal or by a quotation from some universally known service, say "Jackson in F," probably both, combined with contrapuntal ingenuity. This passage should then, by wholly familiar devices, be made to pass over gradually to equally uncompromisingly Catholic music, say the "Adeste Fideles" and a passage of Gregorian plain-song. There should then be an umbrella theme. This would not be difficult; thus, find a theme that could be made to expand or contract — in other words, to open and shut — by augmentation or diminution, by dynamic changes or by ingenious harmonic devices suggesting the most obvious action of an umbrella. Then let this theme fade away, or disappear suddenly, and the umbrella is lost.

Such is the crude outline of a potential masterpiece that should come from the hands of one accomplished in the graphic manipulation of themes in the modern manner. It could even be put forward at first to be listened to "for itself alone, purely as music, without an explanatory programme," as has been done with equally complex and poetic pro-

Programme Music

gramme symphonies before. But it would be well to
see that copious analytical notes were circulated immediately afterwards, in time for the next and all
subsequent performances.

FOLK–SONGS IN AMERICA

THERE was quick response to the note of alarm first raised a few years since about popular songs, folk-songs, and ballads existing in the United States and likely, as such things are all over the world, to die out of the minds of men unless something were done quickly to save them, to preserve them in some permanent way. For a long time there was no general knowledge of their existence. Then many people got to work; and now they are finding, besides the negro songs and the Indian music with which a beginning was made many years ago, ballads, not only in the mountain fastnesses of the Southern Appalachians, but also in more accessible regions of the South, and in the mountains of New England; cowboy songs in the West, Spanish folk-songs in the Southwest. There are organized bands of collectors; college students are out after their prey for doctorate theses; the Indian bureau of the National Government has authorized or sanctioned the work of several skilful and intelligent collectors among the Indians, and has issued their results in Government publications. The Bureau of Education in Washington and various State departments of public education have sponsored bulletins on the subject of popular ballads. The ambulances have all been called out, and have done and are doing all, no doubt, that is humanly possible in the way of rescue. Some day there will come a time of reckoning and accounting as to the value of all this; along with something that has little value, there will no doubt be a good deal that has much.

Perhaps the most remarkable part of all this work, the part that came as a revelation of something new, resulted from the adventures of Howard Brockway, Miss Wyman, Miss McGill, and Cecil Sharp, the English folk-song collector, in gathering what the Appalachian Mountains of the South had to offer. The most experienced of these, and the one who garnered the largest harvest, was Sharp. He had worked long in England in the art of folk-song collecting. This art is not for everybody. It consists in gaining the confidence of folk-singers and persuading them to yield their store of traditional songs, never written down—and indeed the singers often can neither read nor write plain English, to say nothing of the musical notation—and then in noting down accurately what is heard, preserving its peculiarities in speech and music; its rhythms, its intervals, its modal characteristics—all, in short, that goes to make folk-song what it is.

Unfortunately, the noting down of songs from

the mouths of singers requires a special musical knowledge and tact; a technique derived from long experience with this particular task. It is likely that the amateur collectors whose interest has been so greatly aroused in the South, and elsewhere, and who have accomplished so much of value in certain directions, have had and will have more or less difficulty with the music. The music to which these ballads are sung is, nevertheless, of quite as much importance and interest as the words. Most of the literary men who have devoted themselves to this subject have had little knowledge of music and have been little concerned with it in their work. Professor Child himself, in his great collection of English and Scottish popular ballads, sought only for printed or manuscript records of ballads extant or once extant in England and Scotland, and paid practically no attention to the music. In his work it was doubtless out of the question. Collectors from the mouths of the people have learned to pay as much attention to the music as to the words, as the folk-singers themselves do. Sharp relates that time and again, when he asked a singer to repeat words that he failed to catch perfectly, the answer was often given that he could not remember the words without the music; in his mind they were quite inseparable. To recall

Folk-Songs in America

the words he had to sing the ballad. Mr. Sharp went so far as to say that the tunes suffer less by being presented alone than the words: in some cases the omission of the text is an actual advantage, as, for instance, with those old ballad airs that have been divorced from their own proper words—sometimes because they are improper words—and are nowadays allied to modern verses of very small literary value.

Besides the problems that are ordinarily met with by amateurs untrained in the noting down of melodies presented to them through the ear—owing to the lamentable lack of attention to what the French call *solfège* in our musical education—there are special problems offered by a certain proportion of old English and other folk-tunes. One of them is connected with the modal characteristics of such tunes. They are in neither the major nor the minor scale of modern music, but in one of the old ecclesiastical modes that have in some cases survived in them and nowhere else. The folk-tunes show modal influences of the Dorian, Mixolydian, and Aeolian modes, besides the modern major and minor, which often enough occur; they also show the pentatonic scale, and sometimes other "gapped" scales. The Dorian mode is heard when the white keys of the pianoforte are played beginning with D; the Mixolydian beginning with G; the Aeolian beginning with A; the pentatonic scale is heard by playing the black keys in succession, the result being the omission of the fourth and the seventh, or "leading" note. The substitution of the flat for the sharp seventh of the leading note is a characteristic, it will be seen, of the three modes mentioned. In folk-tunes other "gapped" scales than the usual pentatonic scale (characteristic of some of the oldest Scottish tunes) occur. Most musicians whose attention has not been specially directed to these things are apt to try to suppress these modal characteristics and turn the tune into ordinary major or minor. This has been done in the past with many of the transcriptions of Scottish and Irish tunes offered to the public. One of the reproaches made against Thomas Moore for the way in which he presented Irish tunes is that he allowed or encouraged his musical collaborators to "iron out" some of the most characteristic features of those tunes into modern conventionalities. "The Beggar's Opera" has been the source of a good deal of anguish to modern folk-song collectors. As is generally known, the tunes in this opera are mostly old folk-tunes that Gay and Dr. Pepusch got together and fitted to Gay's words. But they were both townsmen; and by one or both of them the modal characteristics of these country tunes were done away with; and, charming as so many of them are, they do not properly represent the form in which the folk-singers used to sing them. If they did, the opera would now be, as it is not, a mine of information to folk-song experts, containing as it does numerous songs that have become obsolete in the mouths of the people.

One of the first to call public attention to the riches in British folk-song that lay unworked among the people of the Southern mountains was Professor C. Alphonso Smith, who wrote in 1915 of "Ballads Surviving in the United States." He laid much stress on the need of immediately rescuing what was still to be rescued and preserved. Knowledge of the ballad was dying out among the younger generation. There is an increasing unwillingness among illiterate people to admit a familiarity with these songs. He tells of one woman who, when asked about ballads, said, "I ain't got no time to be studyin' about them old songs and don't know none of 'em nohow." But she was proud of her familiarity with Moody and Sankey songs; the ballad allied her with a remote and unspiritual past that she wished to forget. Another told her visitor that she had "prayed to

the Lord to take them fool songs out of her mind."
Even worse than this has been the entrance into this
field, with the growth of "schooling" and other
modern improvements, of the "coon songs," jazz,
and other products of Broadway. Everything con-
spires to the destruction of the remaining balladry.

How recent is the interest and the knowledge
that has resulted from it in the collection of ballads
in the South is shown by what Professor George L.
Kittredge of Harvard wrote in his preface to a condensation of Child's great work that he published
in 1904:

"Ballad making, so far as the English speaking
nations are concerned is a lost art; and the same
may be said of ballad singing. A few of the ballads
in Mr. Child's collection are still in oral circulation,
but most of them are completely forgotten, or are
known only in versions derived from print."

Mr. Kittredge has now corrected this statement
in the following manner:

" When I wrote, 'the same may be said of ballad
singing,' I was, of course, in error. Ballad singing is
by no means a lost art, either in Great Britain or
the United States. The evidence for its survival has
come since I wrote. If I were now summing up the
facts, I should modify my statement."

Folk-Songs in America

It is interesting to know what Mr. Sharp himself found in a manuscript collection of a zealous student, the late Mrs. J. C. Campbell, submitted to him in the summer of 1915. The collection was made in the vicinity of Asheville, N. C. It indicated that a vein had been tapped which, if properly and scientifically explored, would yield results, musical, historical, literary, of the first importance. "The ballads in question," wrote Mr. Sharp in his account of it, "were evidently of Irish, Scottish, or English origin, which had presumably been carried to that district by the original settlers and passed down by oral tradition to their descendants, and so, generation by generation, to the present inhabitants. I did not light upon one which was wholly unknown to me, but the collection contained many interesting and illuminating variants of ballads which have been recently noted down by members of the Folk Song Society, including myself, and also variants of many ballads known to us in the older compilations of Motherwell, Kinloch, Walter Scott, etc., but which, so far as we know, are not now being sung in England or Scotland." It was clear that the airs to which these were sung were of the highest interest to students of folk-music; and a look at the memoranda of them convinced Mr.

Sharp that a great effort should be made to institute a thorough and careful investigation into the musical feature of the problem; and that there was need of haste, in view of the rapid disappearance of the custom of ballad singing.

So far from ballad singing being at the moment a lost art, it was found to be not forgotten, even in the United States. In fact, investigation showed that it might be said to flourish in certain parts of the United States more vigorously than it did in England, where in the last twenty-five years or so a zealous effort has been made to collect among the old people of the country-side the last remains of folk-song that modern ways of life, and especially of education, are crushing out. But in the parts of this country referred to, ballads and songs flourish not only among the very old, but also among the young and middle-aged, with whom it is a spontaneous form of self-expression — as much a part of the people's lives as ever in the past, when the world was younger and less sophisticated. The work of destruction had already been begun, but there was still much left to be saved.

The people in the mountains of North and South Carolina, Tennessee, Virginia, and Kentucky, who have been the chief guardians to-day of the living

Folk-Songs in America

ballads and songs of English folk-music, are direct descendants of British immigrants. They have lived in mountain fastnesses for 125 or 150 years, isolated and in great measure cut off from the rest of the country, which, for the most part, — not entirely, however—has forgotten the ballads and folk-songs it ever knew. They have not only kept up the singing of them; they have kept up, to a certain extent, the making of new ballads and songs, as such things were constantly made, from the days of misty antiquity down. It cannot be said that even the ballad-making is wholly a lost art.

And so, following in the footsteps of several others who had gone to collect these songs, Mr. Sharp came to America in 1915 and again in 1917. He returned from his visit profoundly impressed with the people, their character and, in particular, with the great resources of their folk-song and the vigor and vitality of it. They are unlettered, most of them cannot read or write; but, as was the case with the ballad singers of antiquity, this fact has resulted in the greater cultivation of their memories. From various single individuals Mr. Sharp got 30, 40, 50, and even 100 different songs. He tells of one singer of this stamp in England who knew no fewer than 500.

Musical Discourse

These songs are a part of the life of the Appalachian mountaineer. Sharp took down some from a blacksmith whose phrases were delivered in the intervals of blowing the bellows or hammering hot iron. Another would have some difficulty with a song, saying, "If I were only driving home the cows, now, I should remember it right away." Another would have to go into the house and walk about as if attending to her household duties in order to recall a particular song to her mind. Nor is it the adults alone who know these songs, as is very apt to be the case in England. Sharp got some from children; and he was fond of telling of a little boy of 11, who shyly made his way into the singing company with the explanation that he "always liked to be where there was sweet music."

Many of the songs that Sharp found in the Southern mountains are still extant and sung in England. Many others that he found here have died out there in the mouths of the people and have hitherto been known to investigators only from printed records. To gain a living version of them is to the folk-song expert a matter of great interest and significance; it has the character of a "rich haul." Of course a great number of variants were found. It is one of the distinguishing characteristics of folk-song that a fundamental idea, a widely-spread story, is developed in different places and by different communities in different forms. In the case of the American singers, the change of environment caused some things familiar in the old country but unknown in the new, to fall into forgetfulness. Thus Sharp said that on one occasion he was puzzled by the apparently cryptic mention, in a certain song, of "ninety girls." A comparison with its allied version as sung in England showed that it was originally "nightingales"; but there being no nightingales in America, the word had become meaningless, and had been turned into another which at least meant something in itself to the singers.

One of the remarkable features of Mr. Sharp's quest was to find that these old-time songs existed, not only in the remote and inaccessible mountain regions, as he at first expected, but were come upon in certain other places where it might have been supposed that the destructive influences of modern life had killed them. The seeker, having spent weeks and months among the discomforts of the mountaineers' cabins, sought refuge in one or two spots where there were hotel tables and bath-tubs. He had hardly more to do than go a few miles in a motor car to find the people singing the same sort of tunes in the same sort of way; and the collector's zeal was little checked or hindered. Some of the most notable finds were, in fact, made in or near these haunts of comparative luxury. Herein is indicated what the students of this subject have before observed, the remarkable vitality and persistence of this sort of song. But it cannot be long before the levelling and vulgarizing effects will cause the singers to be ashamed of the old songs, and wish to be "like other people" in singing the popular and ephemeral songs of the day.

Mr. Sharp had a hard time in his two trips to the Appalachian regions. Living conditions are not easy there. Provision for travellers is not luxurious. The diet is not such as effete Easterners or Englishmen are accustomed to; nor are the beds. But there is abundant hospitality for those who appreciate the qualities of their hosts. There is a true courtesy such as is not to be found in all rural regions; and, in the case of many of the old women especially, a stately dignity that contrasts strangely with the meanness of the surroundings. Hospitality, however, did not prevent Mr. Sharp from contracting typhoid fever and passing through the crisis of the disease and convalescence from it in a most unpromising spot. But he came out victorious, with all his notes and a rich body of new experience. He put much of both into his interesting book, " Folk Songs of the Appalachian Mountains," a scientific collection, carefully annotated, and also a more popular collection of songs with pianoforte accompaniment. Mr. Sharp's preface to his book is an engaging account of his experiences, and a glowing estimate of the people. His estimate of their character and of the civilization in which they live, is high. Notwithstanding the typhoid fever, the meals, the beds, and all else, he saw the whole thing through roseate glasses, with the enthusiasm of the successful collector. He made no reserves in writing down his enthusiasm.

Another thing that he found in the mountains was a whole series of country dances such as are and were danced by the rustic people in England. One in particular he found, the "running set," a dance of great complication and length. This is described by Playford in his "Dancing Master," first published in England in 1650 and in many editions thereafter, and in other contemporaneous dance books, but has long been obsolete in England. Sharp had the pleasure of taking it back to England from its last refuge in the valleys of Kentucky, and bringing it to life again in its first home.

Musical Discourse

Sharp was fortunate in the hour of his approach. The end is coming in the Southern mountains, as it is in the English counties. The schools that are being introduced into the remote districts—some of them, though not all—the teachings of many religious sects and, still more fatally, the irresistible oncoming of the coal-miners and the timber-hewers and other industrial evangelists, will kill the singing of the old songs and the dancing of the old dances. Music hall ditties, "coon songs" as manufactured on Broadway (though in this part of the South the negro is almost a complete stranger), fox-trots, and jazz generally take the place of them. The young people begin to be ashamed of them as a mark of old fashion. Still more mistakenly, many of the religious preceptors frown upon them as "worldly"; and so another check is put upon them. It will not be long before the whole face of things is changed.

Fortunately it is probable that Sharp and the others who have been at work there, among them Howard Brockway, Miss Wyman, Miss McGill, have achieved the salvation of the songs that most matter.

The interest aroused by the investigators in the South has had the result of showing that the North has not been entirely denuded of its inheritance of the old ballads. Two American collectors, Mrs. Edith B. Sturgis and Robert Hughes, have found in the hills of Vermont what seem to be genuine survivals of fifty of them. The singers were but few, in one out-of-the-way town—farmers, of "good old Vermont stock." Most of these songs have been found elsewhere in this country and bear obvious relationship with versions found in Great Britain; some are known in England and have not yet turned up here. Only two have not been found in any form; the subject of one and the general musical structure of the other seem to preclude a great age for them.

Mr. Sharp printed only a few of the many hundred songs and variants that he found in the South. The rest of his collection made there he deposited in manuscript in the Library of Harvard College. In the numerous collections made before and since his visits to America, there are doubtless others. Some day, perhaps, a definite "Corpus" of these songs will be made, corresponding in some degree to the great collection—unfortunately of the words only —made by Professor Child. To this will be added the numerous "chanties," many of the most interesting being by American sailors or about American subjects. How far it will seem necessary to go in including the Spanish and Mexican songs taken down

[71]

Musical Discourse

in the Southwestern States, the "cowboy songs," and
work songs of different kinds that more recent and
enthusiastic collectors think they have found and
that seem to belong in many cases to a somewhat
different classification, may remain to determine.

AT THE BACK OF SOME DEDICATIONS

A COMPOSER's dedications necessarily imply much that touches most nearly his life, his friendships, his relations to many people, and his work itself. They are not to be left out of account by students of the lives of musicians. What do not the dedications of Beethoven's compositions tell in regard to his life, the circumstances in which from time to time he was placed, the progress of his friendships, the influences that were brought to bear upon him in one way or another, the relations in which he stood to the Vienna of his time! How carefully are they considered by Thayer, his biographer! In the case of no other composer, perhaps, is there so much significance in these marks of friendly consideration or, in some cases, of patronage by the nobility. The old system of patronage, however, had largely passed away; the passionate independence of Beethoven had been largely influential in sweeping away the last vestiges of it.

By the time the "romantic" composers came upon the scene, it was entirely a thing of the past; and dedications had less relation to that form of gratitude which consists in the hope of favors still to come. It is interesting to consider the bearings of the dedications which three of the great leaders of the "romantic" movement of the first third of the nineteenth century made to each other — Schumann, Chopin, and Liszt. Of the possible combinations, only one is lacking. Schumann dedicated his "Kreisleriana," Op. 16, to Chopin, his "Fantaisie," Op. 17, to Liszt; Chopin dedicated his Ballade in F, Op. 38, to Schumann, his Etudes, Op. 10, to Liszt; Liszt dedicated his sonata in B minor to Schumann; but by some chance, Chopin is the "dedikee," as Robert Louis Stevenson used to call it, of no composition of Liszt's. Yet they were friends and for some time in close personal relations; and Liszt's fervent and generous admiration for the Polish composer is permanently recorded in his brilliant essay upon him and his music, and in his transcriptions of his songs.

It may be said that much is told in these dedications, but that, also, something is concealed behind them. What is told and what is concealed forms an amusing little chapter of the musical biography of the time. The facts that subsisted behind these dedications do not tell a story wholly of brotherly love and complete mutual admiration, or of unanimous striving toward one and the same end. The brethren—and sisters, it may also be said—of the

Some Dedications

romantic period of the 'thirties, 'forties, and 'fifties may have been heading in the same general direction, but there was enough diversion in their aims to add a few more vivacities and stresses to that stormy time.

Chopin owed a heavy debt of gratitude to Schumann, who never showed himself more of a seer and a prophet, a critic in the highest sense, than in his published criticisms of the young Polish composer, from the very beginning of his career. Schumann's first essay as a musical critic, which appeared in the *Allgemeine Musikalische Zeitung* of December 7, 1831, when he was a youth of 21, was entitled "An Opus 2" and was devoted to Chopin's Variations on "La ci darem la mano." In it occurs the historic remark, that has since become a classical *locus* in musical criticism, "Hats off, gentlemen, a genius"; and the whole article seethes with the enthusiasm, the fancy, and gay humor, as well as the artistic insight that were to inform so much of Schumann's critical writings in the years to come. In it, too, is made the first appearance of Florestan and Eusebius, already fully characterized.

Three years later Schumann founded the *Neue Zeitschrift für Musik*, in which he continued for ten years his activities as a musical critic and journalist, with the sympathy and insight, the poetic gift, the generous enthusiasm that stamped him as one of the greatest of his guild. During all this time his enthusiasm was aroused by nobody more than by Chopin. He wrote more articles on Chopin and his music than on any other composer or any other subject. They are all couched in terms that clearly set forth the importance of the man for modern art and disclose an appreciation of his music that has not been surpassed by any who have come later, and that has been ratified in the fullest measure by posterity.

Schumann's correspondence shows equally his admiration and comprehension of this "proudest and most poetic spirit of his time," as he called Chopin. His personal relations with Chopin, on the occasions that brought them together, were likewise a frank expression of the same feelings. His letters wherein he describes their meetings overflow with delight. "And Schumann understood Chopin," as James Huneker wrote, "else he could not have written the 'Chopin' of the ' Carnaval,' which quite out-Chopins Chopin."

No wonder, then, that Chopin should respond to this admiring friendship with the dedication of one of his capital works, the Ballade in F, Op. 38, which appeared in 1840. It is characteristic of Schumann's candor that in writing of it in his *Zeitschrift* he should speak of it as "different" from the first Ballade (in G minor), and as "standing as a work of art below it, yet not less fantastic and intellectual" —"a remarkable piece."

Schumann's "Kreisleriana," Op. 16, which appeared in 1838, being among the works which at that time he regarded as his "best," he intended at first to dedicate to Clara Wieck, not yet his bride. To her he more than half promised them, and she, he intimates more than once in his letters, was in his mind when he was composing them. But when they appeared, they appeared as his tribute of admiration for Chopin.

What Chopin's response was is not on record. According to one of his biographers, Scharlitt, Chopin was noticeably cool towards his German champion; there was more enthusiasm on Schumann's side than on Chopin's. As for the "Kreisleriana," alas, there is every reason to believe that he put no value on Schumann's embodiment of his sentiments in this music, however much he may have prized the sentiments themselves. He cared nothing for Schumann's music, had no sympathy with it, and no understanding of it. He never played it himself in his public appearances as a virtuoso; it was not to be found on his desk or on his pianoforte. He never gave it to his pupils to study. When Schumann sent him once a finely bound copy of his "Carnaval" upon its publication in 1837—that "Carnaval" containing the exquisite movement interpreting Chopin's own spirit —his only comment upon it was, "How beautifully they get up these things in Germany!" And when Schlesinger, the Paris publisher of many of Chopin's own works, was thinking of undertaking the publication of the "Carnaval" in France, Chopin advised him that the "Carnaval" was not music at all!

The personal relations between Chopin and Liszt had been of the closest in their earliest years together in Paris; but they cooled. "We are friends; we were comrades," said Chopin in 1842. Of a circumstance that occurred in the course of one of Liszt's amorous escapades and that shocked his fastidious taste and severed their relations, he said that he could not forget that nor certain other things; and that he was much better as he was, with their intimate relations severed. He thought at one time that Liszt had written newspaper articles unfavorable to him; and Liszt's colossal successes as a concert virtuoso so far surpassed his own that there may well have been a feeling of jealousy and resentment. When he heard that Liszt intended to write an account of one of his concerts in a musical journal, Chopin is said to have remarked with a certain bitterness, "He will give me a little kingdom in his empire." Liszt's great essay on Chopin was not published till 1852, three years after his death.

Yet Chopin could not but feel a profound admiration for Liszt's playing. He was delighted with his performance of the Etudes, Op. 10, that he dedicated to Liszt in 1833, and declared that he "wished he could rob him of it." He said to one of his pupils, 'I like my music when Liszt plays it." But he did not like Liszt's music; he played it and taught it no more than he did Schumann's. It should not be forgotten, however, that many of Liszt's more ambitious and seriously intended compositions were not written till after Chopin's death in 1849. What Chopin knew were chiefly the brilliant operatic paraphrases of Liszt's virtuoso days, some of his songs and his transcriptions of songs; and the bad taste in which many of these abound displeased Chopin. Dedications of such things to Chopin would have been obviously incongruous; and there are no dedications by Liszt to Chopin.

The relations of Robert Schumann and Clara Wieck, afterwards Mme. Schumann, with Franz Liszt underwent a marked change in the years between their first meeting, about 1838, and the time when Schumann, a broken man, was overtaken by the loss of his reason; and, so far as relates to Mme. Schumann, the time of Liszt's death in 1886. When they first met him, both were enraptured by the magic of his playing, overcome by its brilliancy and power. They were both brought under the spell of his personality also in those years and could not sufficiently admire either the artist or the man. Their letters and diaries are full of him for a time. Schumann's articles about his playing, in the *Neue Zeitschrift für Musik,* were paeans of praise. Schumann was in ecstasies over his performance of his (Schumann's) compositions — yet, as he acknowledged, it was "not always as I had conceived them." Robert and Clara in those years made few reservations about Liszt; but they made some. These reservations increased, especially in the comments of Clara Schumann, as time went on. Her horizon had its limits and she had her prejudices, and when these grew upon her she was a sour person, not to say a bitter. She was a much-tried woman, and much is to be allowed for the experiences of her life. But she was an implacable enemy and never forgave or forgot.

In the first flush of Schumann's admiration he

Some Dedications

dedicated to Liszt his Fantaisie, Op. 17, which appeared in print in 1839. This was the time of their greatest intimacy, when, having been in Schumann's company for a day, Liszt remarked that it seemed to him as if they had known each other for twenty years; and Schumann agreed to it. Liszt had done much for Schumann already. He had played his music in various parts of Europe when no other pianist but Clara Wieck would look at it; and the great authority of his name and the splendor of his playing had given it a consideration it could never otherwise have gained in those days. He had also published an enthusiastic essay about Schumann and his music at a time when he was personally unacquainted with him (in the *Gazette Musicale*, 1837). Schumann appreciated both and was flattered by them.

Liszt acknowledged the dedication of Schumann's "Fantaisie" with these words: "It is a work of the loftiest kind. I am indeed proud of the honor you do me in inscribing to me a composition of such grandeur. So I wish to work at it and penetrate it thoroughly in order to make with it all the effect possible." And that these were not mere formal expressions of politeness his whole subsequent attitude towards Schumann's music testifies.

Musical Discourse

Liszt naturally responded in kind, with a dedication of his own; but he waited, perhaps, a little too long. His sonata in B minor was published in 1854, inscribed to Robert Schumann. But the Schumanns had long since changed their minds about Liszt, his personality, his compositions, even his playing. There had also been an unfortunate estrangement over an incident of no great importance, that occurred in discussion in a social evening, though it had been patched up.

Before its publication Liszt had played his sonata to Schumann, and his account of it is grim. Liszt was visiting Düsseldorf, where the Schumanns were living—it was probably in 1853—and paid them a visit. Clara played something; and Liszt, who had brought with him the manuscript of his sonata, played it in his turn. He recounted his experience thus:—

"I played it to him once, quite passably. Schumann listened to it at the piano, reading it. He did not know at all what to make of it. At the *adagio* he began to back away, and when I was through he was at the door!"

This being the state of Schumann's feelings, it may occur to some to wonder why Liszt chose precisely this sonata to dedicate to him. The answer

[82]

would be, probably, that he wished to do the greatest honor he could to one whom he had valued so highly, and that he considered his sonata to be one of his most important compositions for the pianoforte.

The sonata was published and came to Mme. Schumann after her husband had been sent to the sanitarium, where he spent the last years of his life in hopeless insanity. Brahms played it to her and she records her impressions of it, and of some other of Liszt's compositions that came with it:—

"The things are awful ! Brahms played them to me, but they made me quite miserable. . . . It is only meaningless noise—not a healthy idea in them, everything confused, not a clear harmonic progression to be found. And now I must write to thank him for it—it is really terrible!"

Liszt's efforts on behalf of Schumann's music, however, were never relaxed; and as Liszt's biographers take some pleasure in pointing out, the Schumanns were perfectly willing to accept his kind offices in producing Schumann's opera of "Genoveva" at Weimar, when it made a failure elsewhere, and in other matters. Mme. Schumann never changed her attitude toward him, however, except to dislike him more. She refused to take part in a musical festival because Liszt was to conduct in it; and she even remained away from the unveiling of her husband's monument in Zwickau, his birthplace, simply for the reason that Liszt was to be present! The crown of her achievement in this direction was reached, however, when the great complete edition of her husband's works was begun by Breitkopf & Härtel in 1886. She was, not unnaturally, appointed editor of the undertaking, and in that capacity, thirty years after her husband's death, she erased his dedication of the Fantaisie in C, Op. 17, to Franz Liszt; and it stands to-day, in the definitive edition of his works, without the inscription that the composer put upon it!

Decidedly, the dedications of these three romantic leaders to one another do not tell the whole story.

WAGNER AND BRAHMS
ON EACH OTHER

WHEN Wagner made the remark about Brahms that in his "Triumphlied" he had "put on the Hallelujah perruke of a Handel," he added one more to a long series of inept and ill-natured comments from his pen upon modern and contemporary musicians, and especially upon Brahms. German composers who were in danger of becoming too universally admired and beloved by the great German public, not to speak of a greater public beyond the borders of Germany, he looked on askance. There is Schumann, for instance, whom he frequently went out of his way to attack; the most notorious instance being an article in the *Bayreuther Blätter* in 1879. The voice was Josef Rubinstein's, but the hands were generally supposed to be the hands of Wagner. The hands of Wagner, at any rate, openly do Schumann shameful violence in the essay "On Conducting." It is hard to believe now that Schumann and Wagner were once considered to be rival leaders of the same school of "new German" music; but criticism of seventy years ago — though perhaps not the best informed criticism of the time — is full of this notion. Wagner was not willing to suffer any rival or even any companion in the field of music. His attitude is suggested by that much-resented remark that he made after the first "Ring" performance at Bayreuth: "at last there is a German art"—the impression being deep and widespread that a German art had already existed. Of course there was immediate explanation and interpretation of the remark as really meaning something else; but it was obviously—perhaps naturally in the first exultation at the realization of a long-cherished dream—what Wagner really thought.

Schumann had definitely stood sponsor for Brahms when Brahms's first works were published in the year 1853; in that year appeared Schumann's famous article, "Neue Bahnen," hailing the coming of a new voice in music. Brahms published his first symphony in 1877. This was, for those who were looking for challenges, a direct challenge added to the old one of Schumann, to Wagner, who had issued the dictum that the symphony had reached its consummation in the Ninth of Beethoven, and that there should be no more symphonies; their place was to be taken by "the art work of the future," his own music dramas, in which all the arts were fused.

It was not to be expected of Wagner that he, a musician whose whole musical nature and whose whole conception of music were so diametrically opposed to everything that was an ideal to Brahms, should have the least patience with his productions, or should, indeed, have much comprehension of them. It was also not to be expected that one whose first impulse was to come out into the open and fight for what he believed and against what he did not believe, and who had such a fluent and forcible controversial style, should rest content with seeing Brahms make his way, even though slowly, with a steadily increasing portion of the public. It was a period of contention; and Wagner lay about him vigorously at this, as he had at other provocations. He let fly freely at Brahms in the stream of essays that still came from his pen as they did in his earlier days when he stood more nearly alone, and as they did almost till the end of his life. This was to be expected. What is less easy to accept is the method of innuendo, sneer, and covert allusion that marks Wagner's course toward Brahms.

Wagner pays his respects to "Herr Johannes Brahms" in a passage of his essay "On Conducting," published in 1869, when Brahms was only just getting a place in the attention of the musical world and had published, besides numerous songs and pianoforte pieces, no symphony, but several chamber music works, the two orchestral serenades, and

"A German Requiem." In this essay Wagner laments the disappearance of "our great and glorious German music" and views with suspicion certain persons "who are treating themselves, and trying to get others to treat them, as keepers and guardians of the sterling 'German' spirit." Brahms was one of these persons. Wagner goes on to say that Brahms "was once so kind" as to play him a set of his " very serious variations"—the variations on a theme by Handel are meant—which showed that "he understands no jokes." In itself, he, Wagner, thought the set excellent. But he did not like Brahms's pianoforte playing. "His performance of other pianoforte music at a concert gave me less pleasure. I even thought it impertinent that the friends of the gentleman professed themselves unable to attribute anything beyond extraordinary technical power to Liszt and his school, whilst the execution of Herr Brahms appeared so painfully dry, inflexible, and wooden. I should have liked to see Herr Brahms's technique anointed with a little of the oil of the Liszt school."

Max Kalbeck, in his "Life of Brahms," gives another account of this meeting between Wagner and Brahms that resulted in the reference to Brahms in the essay "On Conducting." It was in 1864, when

Wagner and Brahms

Wagner invited Brahms, with other musicians, to his "luxurious lodgings," and asked him to play. A listener who long afterwards published his recollections of the occasion (Gustav Schönaich) recalls the excellent playing by Brahms of other compositions by different composers, and the warm enthusiasm with which Wagner overwhelmed him with praise; and in how convinced a manner he spoke about all the details of the Handel variations. "We can see," he concluded his remarks, "what can still be done in the old forms, when some one appears who knows how to treat them." Later, when he came to write "Ueber das Dirigieren," he had changed his mind—evidently.

All in all, it seemed to Wagner (he goes on to say in this essay) "an enigma" that "Brahms could be mistaken for the figure, if not of the Saviour Himself, at least of His best beloved disciple." The taste of this remark has not gained acceptability in the years that have elapsed since controversy raged so furiously as to result in such language. Although it had not much to do with the subject of conducting, with which he was engaged, Wagner says, a little later, in speaking of the "sect" into whose membership he put Brahms: "The 'Liebeslieder Waltzes' of St. Johannes, however odd their name may sound,

[89]

might still be classed among the religious exercises of the lower grade"; a remark carrying out further the peculiar tastefulness of allusion just quoted.

In 1879 Wagner made in his *Bayreuther Blätter* another reference to Brahms, who had in the meantime steadily, though slowly, enhanced his reputation in Germany, and still more slowly outside of Germany. "I know renowned composers you shall meet, to-day at concert masquerades, in garb of street minstrel, to-morrow in the 'Hallelujah' perruke of Handel, the day after as a Jewish tuner-up of Csardas, and later as solemn symphonists, disguised as Number Ten." The chance was too good to be lost—though perhaps it may seem less good at this distance of time—and anything was material for weapons in the hand of Wagner, the polemic with a chip on his shoulder. He meant the "Hallelujah perruke of Handel" to refer to the passages of Brahms's "Triumphlied" in which the chorus hymns a mighty hallelujah for the victory of the German arms over the French in 1871; but he is really a little unfair in calling it a "Handelian perruke"; for it is not a pedantic imitation of the Handelian manner. The "Jewish tuner-up of Csardas"— though why Jewish?—is the Brahms who delighted in the Hungarian pieces that he heard the Hunga-

rian bands play in the Viennese cafés, and who transcribed many of them in the "Hungarian Dances"
for pianoforte duets, so greatly popular—and hence,
it may be inferred, so greatly disturbing to Wagner. The "solemn symphonist disguised as Number
Ten" is, of course, the composer of Brahms's first
symphony, which Bülow called "the tenth"—"but
not as though it should be put after the Ninth of
Beethoven."

In the periodical essays of Wagner's later years,
put forth still in the *Bayreuther Blätter* from the
fastness of Wahnfried, there are some open and
numerous covert allusions to Brahms; the latter
kind Wagner's translator, William Ashton Ellis,
has been at the pains to identify in his edition of
Wagner's prose works. It is rather amusing to see
how the polemical Wagner continued to harp on
the same string about a subject that was evidently
so disagreeable to him, the slow but steady growth
of the acceptance of Brahms's works. In the essay
on "Operatic Poetry and Composition" he suggests
the favorite idea, for a time so industriously exploited by those who took their cue from Wahnfried, that Brahms is preëminently a plagiarist. In
Mr. Ellis's eccentric English it reads: "Our great
symphonists of the 'now-time' might be counselled

to turn any doubt as to the ownership of their stray ideas into downright certainty, before others do it for them." In "Music Applied to the Drama" this entertaining passage is labelled "Brahms" by Mr. Ellis:

"In our symphonies and that sort of thing all now goes world-distraught and catastrophic; we are gloomy and grim, then mettlesome and daring; we yearn for the fulfilment of youthful dreams; demonic obstacles encompass us; we brood, we even rave; and then the world-ache's tooth is drawn, we laugh and humorously show the world its gaping gum; brisk, sturdy, blunt, Hungarian, or Scotch — alas, to others dreary."

And again Wagner speaks of "a certain clammy cast of melody which its creators had transplanted from their heretofore retiring 'chamber music,'" — for Brahms, it will be remembered, had put forward much chamber music for twenty-four years before he was willing to let his first symphony appear. "What had previously been dressed as quintets and the like, was now served up as symphony; little chips of melody, like an infusion of hay and old tea-leaves, with nothing to tell you what you are swallowing but the label 'best,' and all for the acquired taste of world-ache." All of which is in the best style of the propaganda against Brahms, who was supposed to be a gloomy pessimist in his music; and, indeed, whose music was by some interpreted as a lament over his own musical impotence. No doubt this sort of thing furnished the suggestion and starting-point for a certain amount of the anti-Brahmsian literature for several decades.

Again, in the *Bayreuther Blätter* Wagner remarks, perhaps in an anti-Semitic outburst, though Brahms was not a Jew, upon "the great storm that threatened Europe from Asia," and expressed the opinion that it would result in no good. "For it will happen to us here, as it happened after the Aryan migration, when the world preserved only a few of Sophocles's and Aeschylus's tragedies, but, on the other hand, most of Euripides's. Correspondingly, our descendants will have preserved, as against perhaps nine of Brahms's symphonies"—the estimate is, of course, pessimistically prophetic or conjectural—"at the most, two of Beethoven's; for the copyists always go with progress." (Such is Mr. Ellis's translation. Clearness was not a prevailing characteristic of Wagner's style, as this paragraph shows.)

In still another elegant extract from the *Bayreuther Blätter* we may see how Wagner, without naming Brahms, imputes to him, again somewhat obscurely, the composition of the "last thought" of Schumann — did he mean by this "last thought" the essay, "Neue Bahnen," welcoming Brahms as the coming composer? — and the blame of "wishing to compose better than he could, with the purpose of ruining judgment in art and taste in music, misleading managers, directors, and personnel, in order to snatch Hamburg festival banquets and Breslau doctors' diplomas, and take good money from honest people for bad stuff." The genial and kindly references here, so far as they are now explicable, seem to relate to the honor done to Brahms by his native city of Hamburg in 1878, at the fiftieth anniversary of the Hamburg Philharmonic Society, and to the further honor done him by the University of Breslau in 1880 by making him a Doctor of Philosophy, in recognition of which he composed the "Academic Festival Overture."

It was quite in accordance with Brahms's character that he should receive the Wagnerian pinpricks, and sometimes poker-thrusts, in silence; and also that his opinion of Wagner's music should be entirely uninfluenced by any personal feeling towards its composer. Brahms had little literary gift; he never published a line himself; he wrote no articles, so far as is known; carried on no periodical to make propaganda for his music, and entered into no public controversies. A few allusions to Wagner in his letters make up the sum of his known written utterances about Wagner; as in a letter to Simrock, his publisher, where he jocosely compares his own love of fine bindings to Wagner's predilection for silk pajamas; or in one to Bernard Scholz, accompanying the sending of his Serenade, Op. 18, of which he was especially fond, saying he had cherished secretly a sort of Wagnerian idea of writing something very long and beautiful about his fine opus — "but the desire has long since vanished." Brahms himself was a less contentious personality than Wagner; much less articulate about his art and his artistic theories; and on the whole, doubtless, a man of broader mind and wider sympathies. He never had any such revolutionary message to give the world as Wagner, never had to fight for the acceptance of his ideas—at any rate, never did fight for them, but sat down and waited till the world came to his point of view. He found no occasion to excite himself about Wagner's work, even though he might have seen it advancing ever more victoriously on a divergent path that led it farther and farther from his own. But he had a very clear understanding of Wagner's music and of its significance for the modern world. He had studied it deeply and had no hesitation in avowing that fact, and in expressing his opinion of the value of certain of the music-dramas.

"Tristan" he did not like; but he had a high opinion of "Die Walküre" and "Die Meistersinger." In 1855, "Eine Faust Ouvertüre," then recently published in a revised version, "decidedly did not please me," as he wrote to Clara Schumann. He once said to a German writer, Richard Specht, "Do you not suppose that I am the musician who best understands Wagner's works to-day and, at any rate, better than any of his so-called disciples, who would like nothing better than to poison me? I once said to Wagner himself that I was to-day the best of the Wagnerians. Do you suppose I am so limited that I cannot be delighted with the humor and the greatness of 'Die Meistersinger'? Or so disingenuous as to conceal the fact that I consider a few bars of this work worth more than all the operas that have been composed since?"

Brahms had changed his mind about "Die Meistersinger," however, when he said that. In 1870, when the comedy was still new, he wrote to Clara Schumann: "I am not enthusiastic about it —

neither for this work nor for Wagner in general. But I listen to it as closely as possible—as often as I can stand it." Apparently the listening did him good. One thing he rejoiced in, as he says in this same letter: "In everything else I undertake I tread on the heels of my predecessors, which is a hindrance to me. Wagner would never hinder me from undertaking an opera with the greatest relish."

A story was told by Richard Heuberger, to whom Brahms gave some instruction in composition, in 1878. He was expatiating to his pupil on the need of writing legibly, and pointed out, in the autograph score of "Tannhäuser," which he possessed, how careful Wagner was in certain minutiæ of handwriting. "If such a man," said he, "can write neatly, you must do so too." When Heuberger remarked on the responsibility that must be put on Wagner for the confusion prevailing in the minds of young people, Brahms cried out, as if he had been stung, "Nonsense! the *misunderstood* Wagner has done it. They understand nothing of the real Wagner who are led astray by him. Wagner is one of the clearest heads that ever existed in the world!"

The autograph of "Tannhäuser" just referred to was the occasion of a curious passage between the two men that has been detailed at length in

Brahms's biography. Wagner had given it to Peter Cornelius, or to Carl Tausig, the pianist, "to keep." Tausig, who regarded it as a gift from Wagner, perhaps as a recompense for very considerable sacrifices he had made for him, gave it to Brahms. In 1865 Cornelius wrote to Brahms, that the copy was wanted. Brahms for a long time made no answer; finally he wrote to Cornelius that he wished to keep the manuscript, which he did for ten years. In 1875 he got a letter from Wagner, who needed it, he said, for a new revision of the score; Tausig, he wrote, could not possibly have given it away, as he had only left it with him "to keep" for him. He hoped it would need no more words to induce Brahms to return, "willingly and in a friendly way," something that could have only the value of a "curiosity" for him, while it would be for Wagner's son a valued relic.

Brahms answered that, while he would return it "willingly and in a friendly way," he must be allowed to say a few words. To Wagner's son, in view of his possession of so many other of his father's autographs, this would not be so valuable as to Brahms himself who, while not really a collector, liked to have manuscripts which he valued. He did not collect "curiosities." "Possibly it will be more

agreeable to you if I am not allowed to think I
have given you anything. In that case I would say
that, if you rob my autograph collection of a trea-
sure, it would give me great pleasure if you would
enrich my library with another of your works,
perhaps 'Die Meistersinger.' "

Hermann Levi, who was present when this letter
arrived, reported that Wagner fell into a great rage
and cried, "If a lawyer wrote me such a letter, I
would n't mind; but an artist! . . . ." Wagner's rage
subsided, and he answered thanking Brahms, and
regretting that he could not send him "Die Meistersinger," as he was out of a copy. He could do no
better than send him a copy of "Das Rheingold,"
which he did without waiting for his consent—it
was the finely bound copy which was made for the
Vienna Exhibition. "They have often said that my
music is only theatrical decoration; 'Das Rheingold' has suffered much from this reproach. Yet it
may not be uninteresting, in following the later
scores of the 'Ring' to note that I knew how to form
all sorts of themes from the pieces of theatrical
scenery here planted. From this point of view 'Das
Rheingold' may find friendly consideration from
you."

Brahms acknowledged the receipt of the letter

and the volume diplomatically: saying that he derived great pleasure from the splendid gift, and sent heartfelt thanks. The best and truest thanks he gave daily to the work itself—it did not lie unused in his possession. "Perhaps this part of the 'Ring' is less of a stimulus to the detailed study which the whole of your great work deserves; this 'Rheingold,' however, came through your own hands; and may 'Die Walküre' let its beauty glow brightly so that it may outshine this accidental advantage"; and so on, with more polite words of appreciation.

Brahms had no more personal relations with Wagner. That he deeply regretted never having been to Bayreuth is well known. He half intended to go for the first performances of "Parsifal" in 1882; but he could not make up his mind to do so. He was afraid, not of Wagner but of the "Wagnerians," as he said in a letter to Von Bülow: "I need hardly say that I go in dread of the Wagnerians, who would spoil my pleasure in the best of Wagners." He said to George Henschel, about to set out for Bayreuth to hear the first "Ring" performances in 1876: "I know you will rave about it; and I don't blame you. I have to confess that 'Die Walküre' and 'Götterdämmerung' have a great hold upon me. For 'Das Rheingold' and 'Siegfried' I do not particularly care. If I

40612

only knew what becomes of the ring, and what Wagner means by it!" It must be said in extenuation of Brahms's ignorance that the philosophy of "Der Ring des Nibelungen" had not, in 1876, been so extensively elucidated, from Von Wolzogen down to Bernard Shaw's "Perfect Wagnerite" and beyond, as it is now, when all who run may read what becomes of the ring and what Wagner meant by it.

Whatever in Wagner's works Brahms may have liked or disliked, he never, so far as any of his letters or the memories of his friends show, evinced anything like envy of him, or indeed of any other contemporary; nor undertook to belittle his work or denounce his theories, which led so far from his own practice. The wreath which Brahms sent to Bayreuth on Wagner's death in February, 1883, was not a mere decorous compliance with custom, but a sincere tribute of recognition from one great master to another. And however brusque and unpolished—in a word, "bad"—Brahms's personal manners were on occasions when he was ruffled, he never found occasion to put down in writing, even in his private letters, so far as they have been disclosed to the public, anything in the remotest degree as unmannerly as Wagner's published remarks about him. That, of course, shows nothing except the contrasted characters of the two men, and perhaps the widely different experiences and trials they had undergone. It has not the slightest bearing upon their music or their diverse tendencies in art. They stand by themselves; and fortunately the public of to-day is able to love and appreciate the work of both, however far asunder they remain.

THE BEGGAR'S OPERA

IT was unfortunate that New York was not given a real chance to savor and enjoy "The Beggar's Opera" in December, 1920, when it was sent over here as a result of its huge success in London in an out-of-the-way theatre in Hammersmith—a success that carried it through three years there. In New York it was given in a half-hearted way and unskilfully managed, also in an out-of-the-way theatre; and though the cast numbered some of the successful singing actors of the London production, the orchestra was scandalously incompetent to give any account whatever of Frederic Austin's admirable and tasteful rearrangement and amplification of the original score.

Nobody then living in New York, of course, had heard "The Beggar's Opera," except those who had had that good fortune in London. Probably nobody could remember a decrepit and mutilated performance given in 1870 by "a comic opera company under the direction of Fred Lyster" at Wood's Museum and Menagerie. This place of entertainment was in the building afterwards occupied by Daly's Theatre in Broadway, just below Thirtieth Street. "Living curiosities," including dwarfs, as well as dramatic performances, were among its offerings.

Musical Discourse

The English importation appeared at the Greenwich Village Theatre on December 29, 1920. The audience began in the second act to find the performance a charming one, after wondering coolly through the first act at the remarkable differences it showed from comic opera as at present understood in Broadway. It caught up well thereafter and began to find the tunes and dances well worth listening to and encoring, and the sardonic cynicism and bitter flavor of the lines something that could be enjoyed.

"Comic" in the accepted modern sense the opera is not. The satirical intention and the ironical allusions to the manners and customs of the court of George II are still pointed enough to be applicable in George V's time, and to be found amusing; though the thrusts at Sir Robert Walpole are now more elusive, and the burlesque of the Italian opera of Handel's time does not go far enough in the minds of people quite ignorant of that opera to make an impression to-day, even on those ready to receive one. The story itself is one that can still hold together and move forward with a topsy-turvy consistency that some have found Gilbertian; or the original source, perhaps, of the Gilbertian method. Gay hummed the tunes he wanted used to Dr. Pepusch, who set them to the lyrics. They are scattered plenti-

fully through the scenes without too much regard to
the demands of the situation or to the contrasts of
their mood; but they are delightful tunes, as fresh
to-day as they were when they first delighted London. The folk-lorists, indeed, though they may com-
plain of their sophistication by the London townsmen who used them, may well point with pride to
their vitality as folk-tunes. Mr. Frederic Austin's
treatment of the original score has been such as to
let them lose nothing of their character, or of the
semi-archaic flavor which gives them so much of
their charm. The bare indications of the harmony in
the original accompaniments he has developed with
skill and fine musicianship into a fabric of figuration
that adds much to the atmosphere and the insinu-
ating grace of the music. There was much spirit and
humor in the performance as a whole, which hardly
ever suggested the methods and resources of the contemporary comic opera stage. It might be said without offence that it had something of the amateurish;
nor did this seem out of the spirit of the piece.
The stage setting remained practically the same
throughout, minor changes suggesting sufficiently
the very different places in which the action takes
place. Unquestionably the effort made to recapture
"the spirit of Mr. Gay's opera," of which the pro-

gramme made mention, was successful. Curtailment was necessary; and modification of the text for twentieth century taste was also necessary. But this latter was not carried to an undue extent; the flavor still remained high.

It might possibly have surprised the promoters of this English enterprise to learn that "The Beggar's Opera" was first performed in New York, so far as the records show definitely, on December 5, 1750. It was given then by a dramatic company that had come up from Philadelphia, at that time the American metropolis, headed by one Thomas Kean, who was the Captain Macheath, in "a room in Nassau Street that formerly belonged to Rip Van Dam." This was twenty-two years after the original production in London in 1728. It is possible, or even probable, as Mr. Sonneck says in his "Early Opera in America," that it had been performed in New York from 1732 on, in view of the regular intercourse that then went on between London and New York; and the fact that English comedians came to this country and are known to have opened Rip Van Dam's "room" in that year; and that an English ballad opera, "Flora; or Hob in the Well" was given in Charleston, S. C., no later than 1735. If ballad operas in Charleston, why not in New York? At all events,

The Beggar's Opera

"The Beggar's Opera" was given repeatedly in New York and elsewhere in the Colonies from 1750 on, by various companies, and gained a measure of popularity here hardly less than that which it enjoyed in England.

The records show a longer life for "The Beggar's Opera" than has been granted to any other opera, serious or comic. The recent production in London clearly established the fact that the work is still alive to the consciousness of playgoers, and that there was no galvanizing of an operatic corpse— such a galvanizing, it may be whispered secretly, as has been attempted recently more than once in far more majestic and influential quarters in New York.

There was never any question in its early days that "The Beggar's Opera" was intended by Gay as a satire on the profligate manners and customs of the ministers and court of King George II, who had just ascended the British throne; that its immediate motive was resentment at what Gay considered an insufficient offer by the Government of a sinecure office that he had long been seeking; that the ministers of the day, and especially Sir Robert Walpole, were aimed at; and, finally, that all this was expressed by means of a parody on the new fashion of Italian opera imported into London. Sir Robert

Walpole had before that been a target for Gay's satire; but he had the courage to be present at the first night of "The Beggar's Opera" and sat in a stage box. George Hogarth describes the pointed manner in which the audience applied to Walpole the last line in Lockit's song:

> *When you censure the age,*
> *Be cautious and sage,*
> *Lest the courtiers offended should be;*
> *If you mention vice or bribe,*
> *'T is so pat to all the tribe*
> *That each cries, "That was level'd at me!"*

Sir Robert, observing the point and the attitude of the audience, dexterously parried the thrust at the end of the second repetition by calling out "Encore!" in a voice that was audible throughout the house. This produced a "general cheer" from the audience and the song was sung a third time. Nevertheless, the public continued for many years afterward to apply to the famous and notorious minister this line, as well as many other allusions in the opera, so that he never could go to a performance of it with any comfort. The name of Bob Booty, whom Mrs. Peachum inquires about, always raised a laugh at his expense. The quarrel scene between Peachum and Lockit was also understood to refer to a recent quarrel between Sir Robert and Lord Townshend, and kept the audience in a roar on that account.

The notes to Pope's "Dunciad" (written by himself and Swift) say of the first performance and popularity of "The Beggar's Opera": "The piece was received with greater applause than was ever known. Besides being acted in London sixty-three days without interruption and renewed next season with equal applause, it spread to all the great towns of England; it was played in many places to the thirtieth and fortieth time; at Bath and Bristol fifty. It made its progress into Wales, Scotland, and Ireland, where it was performed twenty-four days successively. The ladies carried about with them the favorite songs of it in fans, and houses were furnished with it in screens."

Nor was the fame shed by "The Beggar's Opera" confined to the authors only. The "Dunciad" notes continue in regard to Lavinia Fenton, the first representative of Polly, whose portrait was painted by Hogarth, that "she became all at once the favorite of the town; her pictures were engraved and sold in great numbers, her life written, books of letters and verses to her published, and pamphlets made even of her sayings and jests." And finally she became the Duchess of Bolton.

Musical Discourse

As for Gay, he was a poet of note at the end of the seventeenth and beginning of the eighteenth century; an intimate friend of Pope and Swift and the author of more than one successful play and of the well-known ballad, "Black-Eyed Susan." What brings him to the attention of music lovers particularly, besides "The Beggar's Opera," is his libretto of Handel's serenata, "Acis and Galatea." Dr. Pepusch, his collaborator in setting the tunes, a German who settled in England about 1700, wrote some operas and cantatas, played the organ, taught music, and became an active factor in the English musical life of the time.

For a century, while the piece had what may be called its first vogue, as distinguished from that which has now come to it, there was great argument about the morality and propriety of "The Beggar's Opera." For a long time, according to Michael Kelly's "Reminiscences," the Irish Government prohibited its performance in Dublin. The argument about its morality and propriety was concerned with the question of its subject and treatment. It was one of the matters with which Dr. Johnson and his circle, to whom argument, discussion, and conversation generally were the breath of life, occasionally tussled. There is hardly a volume of the letters of the period but contains a contribution to the criticism of "The Beggar's Opera." Boswell projected a quarto volume, "to be embellished with fine plates," on the subject of the controversy occasioned by it. He reports several of the ambrosial conversations of Dr. Johnson and his friends dealing with the famous subject. Johnson's deliverances upon it were many. One of the most notable was that "there is in it such a labefaction of all principles as may be injurious to morality." After that there would seem to be little to add. But in a more serious vein he thought that more influence was ascribed to the morals of the opera than they really had. "I do not believe any man was ever made a rogue by being present at its representation." He returns to the subject in his "Life of Gay," where he observes that the play was plainly written only to divert, without any moral purpose, and is therefore "not likely to do good."

These things, it must be remembered, were said and written half a century after the opera was first produced, and after it had become a "classic." It was not what Gay himself thought, or at least wrote to Swift: "For writing in the cause of virtue and against the fashionable vices I am looked upon at present as the most obnoxious person, almost, in

England." And Dr. Arbuthnot, writing to the same distinguished correspondent at the same time observed: "The inoffensive John Gay is become one of the obstructors to the peace of Europe, the terror of the ministers, the chief author of 'The Craftsman' and all the seditious pamphlets which have been published against the Government." Boswell himself ventured to disagree with Dr. Johnson: "I should be very sorry to have 'The Beggar's Opera' suppressed, for there is in it so much of real London life, so much brilliant wit, and such a variety of airs which from early association of ideas engage, soothe, and enliven the mind, that no performance which the theatre exhibits delights me more." Boswell reports "an ingenious observation of Mr. Gibbon," that "The Beggar's Opera" may perhaps have sometimes increased the number of highwaymen; but that it had a beneficial effect in refining that class of men, making them "less ferocious, more polite; in short, more like gentlemen"—an ingenious observation indeed, and complimentary in its estimate of operatic moral influence.

Horace Walpole, genial cynic, son of the Sir Robert whose withers were so severely wrung, wrote that "Justice Fielding had revived the hypothesis of 'The Beggar's Opera' making all our rogues.

The Beggar's Opera

Garrick has, in a manner, given it up; but they continue it at Covent Garden. . . . Did you know before that Macheath begot all our nabobs?" As a matter of fact, Sir John Fielding, the Bow Street magistrate, sent letters to the managers of Drury Lane and Covent Garden, advising them not to perform "The Beggar's Opera," " as it tended to increase the number of thieves." That Garrick, manager of Drury Lane, declared himself on Justice Fielding's side and against the opera was uncharitably explained by some as due to the fact that he had but one good singer in his company and was thus handicapped in presenting the opera himself. Coleman, the rival manager, however, answered the Justice that he did not think his the only house in Bow Street where thieves were hardened and encouraged — the point being that Covent Garden Theatre is itself also, like the police court, in Bow Street — and that he would persist in continuing the representation of "that admirable satire, 'The Beggar's Opera.'"

But nobody was more emphatic in his defence of Gay's work than Dean Swift. "Nothing," he wrote, "but servile attachment to a party, affectation of singularity, lamentable dullness, mistaken zeal, or stupid hypocrisy, can have the least reasonable objection against this excellent moral performance of the celebrated Mr. Gay." The original suggestion for "The Beggar's Opera," indeed, is said to have come from Swift, who one day remarked to Gay, "what an odd, pretty sort of thing a Newgate pastoral might make." "Gay," as Pope said, "was inclined to try at such a thing for some time, but afterward thought it would be better to write an opera on the same plan." Swift, who looked at Gay's draft, thought it would not do. Pope reports that neither he nor Swift believed it would succeed, and when they showed it to Congreve he said, "It would either take greatly or be damned confoundedly"; wherein Congreve seems to have played safe as a prophet. Colley Cibber, to whom the opera was first offered, rejected it. Quin, the famous actor, had so bad an opinion of it that he refused the part of Macheath and gave it to Walker, who acquired great celebrity in it.

It was not long after the first appearance of "The Beggar's Opera" that bowdlerization was considered necessary; and changes were also made in the manner of performance such as later were witnessed with amazement during the days of the wild popularity of "Pinafore," a hundred and fifty years later. One of the caprices indulged in was the assignment of the part of Captain Macheath to a woman. Another of the experiments attempted was to give performances of it by children's companies, again foreshadowing some of the queer things done to "Pinafore." A woman was put into Macheath's part in Covent Garden Theatre in 1772; and Mme. Vestris, one of the most popular singers in England in the first years of the nineteenth century, shone for a time as Captain Macheath, though she also took the part of Lucy Lockit in other performances. And in some of the New York performances the records show that women were cast as Macheath. That was not a cause of surprise in those days; for as late as the early years of the nineteenth century such parts as that of Romeo in several different operatic versions of "Romeo and Juliet," and the heroes of numerous other operas, were given to women.

An improvement of the "morality" of the piece, extending beyond the text to the action, was one of the experiments tried upon it at Covent Garden in 1777; no doubt to meet the criticisms passed upon it by Dr. Johnson and by others before and after him. In this version, Macheath is sentenced to hard labor, is visited in prison by both of his "dear charmers," Polly and Lucy, acknowledges the leniency of his sentence, and promises to become a virtuous member of society. It is hardly necessary to say that this homily met with no approval from audiences that knew the work as Gay and Pepusch left it.

William Hazlitt, whose reputation as a dramatic critic the passing of a century has hardly dimmed, was full of admiration for "The Beggar's Opera," and is one of the upholders of its "morality." Among other things he observes that "the exclamation of Mrs. Peachum when her daughter marries Macheath, 'Hussy, hussy, you will be as ill-used and as much neglected as if you had married a lord' is worth all of Miss Hannah More's labored invectives on the laxity of the manners of the time." In another essay he calls it "an inimitable play, uniting those two great things, sense and sound, in a higher degree than any other performance on the English stage or (as far as we know) on any other stage. . . . All sense of humanity must be lost before 'The Beggar's Opera' can cease to fill the mind with delight and admiration." He indulges in some entertaining speculation as to possible representatives of the characters: "We do not know of any actor on the stage who is enough of a fine gentleman to play Macheath. Perhaps the older Kemble might, but

then, he is no singer! it would be an experiment for
Mr. Kean, but I don't think he could do it."

As to the theory that the musical form of the
work is meant as a parody of Italian opera, opinions
have differed as widely as over its morals. Parody
and assault on Italian opera, not long before first
brought to England, were much in vogue since Addison and other wits of the time had made it a
target for ridicule in *The Spectator* and other contemporary literary publications. It seems evident
that the spirit of parody runs through the work.
At any rate, the opera, with its satirical lines and
dramatic situations, aided by Dr. Pepusch's treatment of popular tunes of the day—not all folk-
tunes, for there are others in the score—was more
deadly to Italian opera than all the literary attacks.
"The Beggar's Opera" at the Little Theatre in
Lincoln's Inn Fields, is considered to have been one
of the reasons why Handel's Italian opera at the
King's Theatre, under the auspices of the Royal
Academy of Music, went into bankruptcy. According to the "Dunciad" notes, "it drove out of England for that season the Italian opera, which had carried all before it for ten years." And it ought to count
for something that it gave an opportunity for the
long-lived jest about making Gay rich and Rich gay.

Musical Discourse

Sir John Hawkins, the English historian of music, writing half a century after the first production, could see no parody in "The Beggar's Opera" because it did not conform to his conception of a parody. An operatic parody, he thought, should have "a mean subject, a mock hero, a bombastic style, set in recitative with airs intermixed, in which long divisions are made on insignificant words." Dr. Charles Burney, the rival historian of music, of the same time, was sure that "The Beggar's Opera" was really a burlesque. So, it may be said, was Dr. Johnson, whose opinion was worth less on this matter. Dean Swift, contemporary and friend of Gay, speaks with more authority when he says that "'The Beggar's Opera' exposeth with great justice that unnatural taste for Italian music among us, which is wholly unsuited to our northern climate."

It seems probable that Gay put into his opera the spirit of parody on the Italian opera because the people he was aiming at were chief supporters of that opera. The method was simple. Pepusch used a large number of well-known popular tunes, "folk-tunes," to which Gay set new words, in place of the arias and recitatives of Italian opera. When the moment of emotion or passion arrives, as it does frequently, or even when it is only time for a tune,

a tune is forthcoming; and a study of the text and
the score shows how cleverly Pepusch fitted the
quality of the airs to the sentiments and, still more,
to the character of the people who sing them. The
burlesque effect is introduced when these thieves,
robbers, and street-walkers fall into sentiment and
compare themselves, like operatic heroes and heroines, to flowers, ships, bees, and so on. In one or
two of the songs Pepusch undertakes to mock the
coloratura airs of the opera, as in that sung by
Lucy and Polly alternately, "Why, how now,
Madam Flirt!" ("If you thus must chatter and are
for flinging dirt") where he has put three measures
of the original into "divisions" on the word "dirt"
such as Sir John Hawkins looked for. And this
altercation between the two rivals for Macheath's
affections is considered to be an allusion to the
famous quarrel between Faustina Hasse and Cuzzoni, singers in Handel's Italian company, when
they scratched each other's faces on the stage. The
little orchestral interludes of a couple of measures
in Lucy's song lamenting her hero's fate seem small
because familiar things to us now—yet these very
possibly struck the listeners of 1728 as a burlesque
of the pathetic orchestral interludes in Italian opera.
And in the duet between Polly and Lucy, as they

contest again for Macheath, they literally snatch the words from each other's mouths; so that when it is ended, Macheath not unnaturally asks, "What would you have me say, ladies?"—which is considered by some to mock the difficulty of grasping the text in complicated passages of the serious opera. Some of these things, it must be confessed, are a little far-fetched as points in making out a case for parody; yet some of them seem to count in this direction. Then there is the ballet. There must, of course, be a ballet in opera, and in "The Beggar's Opera" the most unlikely and unfavorable moment is chosen with what seems undeniably burlesque intent. The scene is Newgate; and "the Prisoners whose tryals are put off till next session are diverting themselves." Thereupon there is "a Dance of Prisoners in chains," etc. There is no indication in the original score of what music was used for this dance.

Gay and Pepusch had a rich store of folk-tunes to draw upon. All the airs in the opera, with a few exceptions, though they have lost something of their true and rustic nature, are such folk-tunes. Among these exceptions is, first, the march in Handel's opera of "Rinaldo," to which Matt of the Mint sings the words "Let us take the road," and which is turned also into a chorus in Mr. Austin's

version of the opera—a piece which was popular
in England for many years as "The Royal Guards'
March"; the quotation may be considered, under
the circumstances, malicious. Several of the songs
were brought to London by the Italian singers
from Paris, as "the French tune that Mrs. Slamme-
kin was so fond of," and that inscribed "Cotillon,"
a tune popular in France, which has been traced
to Germany as far back as 1664. It may still be
found in one of Weckerlin's collections of French
popular songs. The drinking song, "Fill ev'ry glass,"
sung by Matt of the Mint, was also one of the Italian
singers' songs. One of the tunes of the opera most
familiar to elderly ladies and gentlemen of the present day who, in times gone by, used to dance the
lancers, is that to which the words "If the heart of
man is depress'd with cares," are sung by Macheath;
for it was the invariable tune for one of the figures
of that dance. It has an ancient history; it is found
in John Playford's "Dancing Master," first published in 1650. More famous but perhaps less familiar is "The Tune of Green Sleeves," which dates,
at the latest, from 1580; it is the tune that Mrs.
Ford makes mention of in "The Merry Wives of
Windsor," saying that Falstaff's words and his disposition "do no more adhere and keep pace to-

gether than the Hundredth Psalm to the tune of
'Green Sleeves.'" In the opera it is one of a long
series of tunes that Macheath sings in the "con-
demn'd hole" before his release to secure a happy
ending for the piece. The rapid section of the overture is based on the tune "Walpole, or the Happy
Clown," which is also used in the opera to the words
"One Evening, Having lost my Way" (omitted in
Mr. Austin's version). This has been considered by
some as a notice to Sir Robert Walpole (the "Walpole" in the much earlier original words of the tune
having, of course, no reference to the famous minister) of what was coming to him, emphasis being
laid on this by the thrice repeated "revenge" at the
close of the song sung by Lucy. If this interpretation be fanciful, it is at least based on a striking
coincidence.

Of the other songs a large proportion can still be
traced in various forms. Several of them are among
those for which George Thomson had accompaniments written by Haydn, Beethoven, Pleyel, and
others for his collection of Scottish and other tunes.
It should be emphasized that probably all the tunes
in the opera were then well known to everybody in
the audience. This fact, no doubt, had a large share
in establishing the popularity of the work.

The Beggar's Opera

"The Beggar's Opera," however, has been something of a thorn in the flesh of the modern folk-song collectors. Although most of the airs in it were derived from familiar folk-tunes, they are, as they stand, not faithful transcriptions of genuine folk-tunes. One of the most usual, and in the eyes of the specialist, one of the most vicious of the changes to which the original airs were subjected in their incorporation into the opera, was the destruction of the "modal" characteristics which frequently belonged to folk-tunes, English and other, especially to the oldest ones. The flat sevenths which should be heard in Dorian, Mixolydian, and Aeolian tunes are turned into sharp "leading tones" in the modern manner, certain dominant cadences are introduced which are inadmissible in the modes, where they do not properly belong; and other changes are made to make the tunes sound "right" to modern ears used to the major and minor modes and unused to any other. (It may be said that the Dorian, Mixolydian, and Aeolian modes are successions of tones found by playing a scale on the white keys of the pianoforte, beginning with D, G, and A, respectively. The sevenths are all flat.)

Cecil Sharp, one of the chiefs of the folk-song authorities, did not find it easy to decide which of the two collaborators, Gay or Pepusch, must be held responsible for what he considers the maltreatment of the traditional airs in "The Beggar's Opera." He thought it could not be Pepusch, because Pepusch was a "first-rate musician"; and, unlike his professional brethren, had a keen affection for, as well as an abstruse knowledge of, the ancient modes, and wrote two books about them. On the other hand, thought Mr. Sharp, it is more than probable that Gay, who was a townsman and therefore steeped in the music of the day, would unconsciously modernize the tunes which he sang to his collaborator to take down and use. "This," says Sharp in his book, " English Folk Song," "is not to accuse him of any want of good faith; not being a technical musician he might easily have altered the air without knowing that he had done so."

Fixing the responsibility at this day is not very easy; nor is it very important. Mr. Sharp's conclusion may be noted: "It is impossible to accept the tunes in 'The Beggar's Opera' as trustworthy records of peasant song; and a like criticism must regretfully be passed upon all the so-called folk-airs contained in the forty or more ballad operas which followed upon the heels of 'The Beggar's Opera.' Had the musicians who were responsible for the

The Beggar's Opera

music of the ballad operas but had the grace to present the tunes in their native dress, unadorned and 'unimproved,' *i.e.*, as the peasantry were at the period singing them, the ballad operas of the eighteenth century would now be of incalculable worth, veritable treasure-houses of English folk-song. As it is, they are but the repositories of tunes which, scientifically speaking— that is, for the purpose of ascertaining and comparing the manner the peasantry really sang them — are well nigh worthless."

It is indeed sad ; but, after all, the authors or compilers of the ballad operas, including the first and most famous of them, were working for success with an audience to whom the Dorian, Mixolydian, and Aeolian modes meant less than nothing and who wanted to hear tunes they all knew, in the way that sounded most natural and familiar. How far Gay and Pepusch succeeded in presenting them so, the " Beggar's Opera's" history of two hundred years shows.

SHAKESPEARE AND MUSIC

SHAKESPEARE lived at a period when England was one of the most musical nations of Europe. Not only did the England of that time produce composers ranked among the greatest, music that could be matched with any that was written anywhere, but also the love and knowledge of music—a practical and often advanced technical knowledge—were widely spread among the upper and middle classes; and among the lower were cultivated in their own naïve and genuinely musical way. Every person claiming any title to education or social position was expected to do his share in extemporaneous part-singing. He was also expected to be able to play at sight, and even to improvise, according to the rules of counterpoint, upon stringed instruments. Attention has often been called to the entertaining manner in which Thomas Morley begins his "Plaine and Easie Introduction to the Skille of Musick," by describing the plight of a young gentleman, meeting some friends, who is unable to join them in the musical diversions they propose and is in consequence looked at askance as a person of imperfect education. It was a matter of course that this musically illiterate young person took immediate steps to remedy his deficiencies, and thus offered a peg for Morley to hang his treatise upon.

Women of the upper classes were generally expert practitioners on the virginals, a smaller sized spinet. The spinet and harpsichord were no strangers to most houses; and it has often enough been explained how a cittern — a four-stringed instrument of the guitar kind — hung in the barbers' shops for waiting customers to play upon, taking thus the place of *The Police Gazette* ; and, like that roseate sheet, considered pretty vulgar in its way. Pepys's "Diary" gives constant illustration of how much a gentleman of a generation or two later than Shakespeare's time concerned himself with music. Pepys was, as he called himself, a " lover of Musique"; but he was hardly an exceptional case — he was far less an exceptional case than such a man would be in America or England to-day.

This universal love and knowledge of music among the people of England — that is to say, among the audiences that listened to Shakespeare's plays at the time when he produced them — are reflected in the plays themselves. There are few of them that do not contain some reference, often many and copious references, to music: some figurative mention of it, if not an allusion to actual music heard; frequent punning plays upon musical terms. Many of such passages are elaborated and have more than a passing significance in the play. The passage about the recorders, in which Hamlet turns upon Rosencrantz and Guildenstern; the punning contest in the second act of "The Taming of the Shrew," between Hortensio and Baptista; Lorenzo's exquisite passages in "The Merchant of Venice," including the allusion to the Pythagorean "music of the spheres"; and numerous others of a similar sort will occur to most lovers of Shakespeare. It is hardly possible to read through any of the plays, especially the comedies, without coming upon some allusion to music.

These facts suggest two things. One is that these incessant allusions to music, and the frequent puns involving technical terms, which have to be explained in the notes for the untaught modern reader, must have been perfectly clear and intelligible to the contemporary audiences. The contemporary audiences would not patiently have put up with so large a measure of dark sayings. The other is that Shakespeare's musical allusions show the same range of knowledge and accuracy as has been noticed in regard to so many of his allusions to other technical subjects, in other branches of art and science. Some of his musical puns may be far-fetched; deplorable, discouraging, considered merely as puns. But they never show a faulty technical knowledge. Music had a place, and an important one, in the "myriad mind" of Shakespeare.

Among the musical allusions in Shakespeare are naturally not a few to songs, contemporary, or of an earlier date. Mistress Ford, in "The Merry Wives of Windsor," observes that Falstaff's disposition and his words "do no more adhere and keep pace than the Hundredth Psalm to the tune of 'Green Sleeves.'" Later in the same play Falstaff calls upon the sky to "thunder to the tune of 'Green Sleeves.'" The tune meant is "A new courtly sonnet of the Lady Green Sleeves," a song of Henry VIII's reign, immensely popular then and later. In "Much Ado About Nothing" Beatrice says that she "may sit in a corner and cry 'Heigh ho for a Husband,'" and there is another mirthful reference in the play to the same old tune. "Heart's Ease" is urgently called for from the musicians in the fourth act of "Romeo and Juliet" by Peter, who wants comfort because his heart itself plays another old tune, "My heart is full of Woe." Twice the tune "Whoop, do me no harm" is mentioned in "A Winter's Tale"; the rest of the words are unknown.

[129]

"Malvolio's a 'Peg-a-Ramsay' and 'Three Merry Men be We,'" says Sir Toby Belch in "Twelfth Night," referring to two old songs so entitled. An amusing use is made of the song " Farewell, Dear Love," in "Twelfth Night," where Sir Toby quotes it line for line in answer to remarks addressed to him successively by Malvolio, Maria, and the Clown. Of this the music was composed by Robert Jones, one of the prominent composers of the Elizabethan period.

There are many such; many scraps of the words of old songs; some quoted entire, some merely alluded to, by their titles, as something that would be familiar to every listener. Of some the words are no longer known. Of others the tunes are not now to be identified. But of the great majority both words and music are known and to be found in collections of such things, as Chappell's "Popular Music of the Olden Time." Some of these are supposed to have accompaniment, some are without. There is a duet, a trio, a chorus, not to mention several rounds, either quoted or alluded to. Dr. Charles Vincent gives a list of thirteen; but there are more. E. W. Naylor mentions thirty-four and says the list is not complete. He gives further many allusions to the names of tunes and catches—at least eighteen or twenty more, the music of which is still known. As to all these songs, the inference is obvious that they were known to most in the audience, and that Shakespeare's references to them were found apt and suggestive and, very often, amusing.

Besides the songs to which he makes so numerous allusions, Shakespeare calls for songs to be sung in many of his plays. These cases are too frequent and many of them are too well known to need more than instancing; such as the "Willow" song in "Othello"; "O Mistress Mine" in "Twelfth Night"; "It was a Lover and his Lass" in "As You Like It," "Where the Bee Sucks" in "The Tempest." There are many more. It is likely that Shakespeare wrote many of these verses—forty-seven songs are listed as being integral parts of the plays —to tunes already existing and popular at the time; but investigators have not arrived at certainty upon this point.

Unfortunately, there are only six songs of which we possess the music exactly as it was sung in the plays in Shakespeare's time. The Globe Theatre was burned in 1613, and with it were lost most of the performing manuscripts, including the music of the songs. Only one of this class of songs was by a composer whose fame has endured—Thomas Morley, who wrote the music of "It was a Lover and his Lass" in "As You Like It," appearing in the first book of his "Ayres or Little Short Songs," published in 1600. Of this book there is only one copy known, which is in the possession of a New York collector. There is some reason to believe that no existing version of this song and its accompaniment is exactly accurate. The accompaniment is written in the lute tablature, the copying and transliteration of which are peculiarly liable to error. Unfortunately, the possessor of this unique volume has not yet found it in his heart to allow students and scholars to examine it in order to establish a correct version.

Robert Johnson, a composer and lutenist of the early seventeenth century, wrote music for "Where the Bee Sucks" and "Full Fathom Five," in "The Tempest," probably for performance in the play during Shakespeare's lifetime. The other four supposed to be contemporaneous and to have been sung as we now possess them, are the "Willow" song in "Othello," "O Mistress Mine" in "Twelfth Night," both by unknown composers; "Lawn as White as the Driven Snow" from "The Winter's Tale," and "Take, O Take those Lips Away" from "Measure for Measure," have no certain attribution.

Musical settings of the songs in the plays are

simply legion in later years. Composers have found them a mine that yields indefinitely, and the list of them grows every year. Shakespeare's songs have always been a strong temptation to composers and began to be, of course, as soon as they were known. Naturally, English composers first turned to them. Henry Purcell, besides his complete opera based on Shakespeare, "The Fairy Queen," adapted from "A Midsummer Night's Dream" composed much incidental music for the plays, as for "Macbeth," and for Shadwell's versions and tinkerings of "Timon of Athens" and "The Tempest." From the latter we possess Purcell's settings of "Come unto these Yellow Sands," "Full Fathom Five" and, for chorus, "Hark, Hark, the Watch Dogs Bark." Even earlier John Banister and Pelham Humfrey found inspiration in Shakespeare. Banister was the chief of Charles II's band of violins; Humfrey, a still greater favorite of that monarch; they collaborated in music for "The Tempest." To enumerate even only the most noted composers and their settings of Shakespearean songs from that time to this would be to compile a catalogue. Dr. Thomas Augustine Arne, composer of "Rule Britannia," among other things, wrote many such settings, some of which are still sung. Sir Henry R. Bishop, most famous now, perhaps, as the composer of "Home, Sweet Home," was remarkably industrious in writing music for the plays and for perversions and rearrangements of them. Sir Arthur Sullivan provided music for "The Tempest," "The Merchant of Venice," "The Merry Wives of Windsor," "Henry VIII," and "Macbeth." Mendelssohn's music for "A Midsummer Night's Dream" is, of course, better known than any other incidental music for Shakespeare's plays. Sir Hubert Parry and Sir Charles Stanford have in later years added to the list of Shakespeare songs.

A few of the most beautiful and most famous Shakespeare songs have come from Germany. Haydn, whose visits to England brought English verses to his attention, set music for "She Never Told Her Love," which is not among the better known of his English songs. It need hardly be said that two of the most perfect and best beloved of Shakespearean settings are Schubert's; best known is probably "Hark, Hark, the Lark" in "Cymbeline," that "wonderful sweet air with admirable rich words to it"; that "very excellent, good conceited thing," as Cloten calls it, when he persuades Imogen to sing it. Unforgettable, too, is the story of its origin, as told by Schubert's friend Doppler: how he was sitting in a beer garden with a friend who had a volume of

Shakespeare and Music

Shakespeare in his hand, which Schubert seized and began to read; and, pointing to the verses, exclaimed, "Such a lovely melody has come into my head," and then and there wrote down on the back of a bill of fare, amid the hubbub of the beer garden, an immortal song. Hardly less popular and widely beloved is "Who is Sylvia?" from "The Two Gentlemen of Verona." The third of Schubert's Shakespearean settings, the drinking song, "Come, thou Monarch of the Vine" from "Antony and Cleopatra," is much inferior to its companions and is correspondingly little known.

It is natural that the operatic librettists, an insatiable tribe, rummaging through all the world's literature for their material, should repeatedly have laid violent hands upon the plays. These have served as a basis for more operas than the works of all the other great poets put together. Shakespeare, however, has had his revenge upon almost all the librettists and composers who have dared to touch him. The quality and substance of the plays have rarely failed to plant the seeds of more or less speedy death in any perversion of them. Not till the true spirit of the lyric drama came to the consciousness of both composer and librettist was it possible to make a Shakespearean opera that had the breath of life in it and that was in any essential other than an indignity to a great genius and a maltreatment of a masterpiece. This achievement was made by an Italian, with the invaluable and indispensable aid of another Italian, both of whom assimilated the spirit and meaning of Shakespeare as no other dramatic composer and librettist before them had ever done. They were Giuseppe Verdi and Arrigo Boito; and their joint works, "Otello" and "Falstaff," are to-day practically the only Shakespearean operas that really represent in the lyric drama the full significance of their great prototypes.

It is not from want of trying that innumerable masterpieces in Shakespearean opera have not been produced. The first of a great number appears to have been Henry Purcell's "Fairy Queen," based on "A Midsummer Night's Dream." The libretto was adapted by an anonymous writer, and the opera was first played in 1692. One peculiarity of the libretto is that not a single line appears as Shakespeare wrote it, with Purcell's music. The score was lost in 1700 and a reward was offered for it in that year. By an extraordinary turn of events, it was found in the library of the Royal Academy of Music in London, in 1901; and has since been published.

Perhaps the first of a long and venturesome line

of musicians outside of England to evolve a real opera out of a play of Shakespeare was Francesco Gasparini, whose "Ambleto" — the Italian idea of the name Hamlet — was, according to Burney, "written by Apostolo Zeno and set for the Venetian theatre in 1705," and was produced at the Haymarket in 1712. But, adds Burney, "there is very little resemblance in the conduct of this drama to Shakespeare's tragedy of the same name, though both seem to have been drawn from the same source, the Danish history by Saxo Grammaticus." It seems likely, however, that Shakespeare was better known in Venice in 1705 than Saxo Grammaticus. "The overture to 'Hamlet,'" says Burney, "has four movements, ending with a jig. . . . Signora Isabella has a noisy song for trumpets and hautbois *obligati* in 'Hamlet'; in Margarita's songs there are many passages of *bravura;* and the airs of Mrs. Barbier, who sings in the contralto, are chiefly pathetic. There are few songs, however, in this opera which would please modern judges of Music" —*i.e.*, in 1789—"either by their melody, harmony, or contrivance." Another "Amleto" — so spelled this time — and one of a number from Italy in the early eighteenth century, was by Domenico Scarlatti. It was first given in Rome in 1715; and though its composer is known to all musical amateurs as the composer of harpsichord pieces in great numbers, that still live and are enjoyed, "Amleto" has long since gone to the limbo that was awaiting other operatic "Hamlets." Of these a considerable number appeared in Italy in the latter half of the eighteenth and early years of the nineteenth centuries and have completely disappeared. Perhaps the last considerable Italian version was one by Franco Faccio, who wrote to a text by Boito. Faccio was one of the foremost conductors of his time in Italy—he directed the first European performance of "Aida" and the first production of "Otello," both at La Scala in Milan. But this fact and Boito's collaboration has not saved his opera, which is forgotten now except for an aria or two occasionally sung.

Max Maretzek, known for many years in New York as a conductor and impresario, wrote a "Hamlet," which was produced in 1843, in Europe, five years before he came to America. The one "Hamlet" that is still known is Ambroise Thomas's, a French "Hamlet, produced at the Opéra in 1868, whose libretto, by Barbier and Carré, responsible for many things of the kind, is a shocking and foolish perversion of the great tragedy. It has been

heard recently in New York, not because anybody
wanted to hear it, but because Titta Ruffo wanted
to sing the title part, and " baritone's operas" are
not abundant. But it is a soprano's opera, too; and
Emma Calvé, in 1893, the year of her first appearance in New York, made much of the part of
Ophelia,' as did Marcella Sembrich and Christine
Nilsson and other great sopranos before her.

Better known to opera-goers of the present day,
and somewhat less injurious to the source from
which it is derived, is Gounod's " Roméo et Juliette," the libretto of which was written by the same
ruthless pair of collaborators, Barbier and Carré.
More than almost any other play of Shakespeare,
"Romeo and Juliet" offers appetizing material to
composers and librettists, and they have not neglected it. The last adaptation of it that preceded
Gounod's was "I Capuleti ed i Montecchi" of
Bellini, first disclosed in 1830. It soon gained great
popularity, owing partly to the singing in it of
Giuditta Pasta, for whom, though a soprano, curiously enough, as it seems in these days, the part
of Romeo was written, and of Grisi as Giulietta
and of Rubini as Tebaldo, a character considerably
more prominent in the opera than in the play. In
that historic operatic season of 1825–26, when

Manuel del Popolo Garcia brought his family to New York, and with them Italian opera for the first time in the New World, he produced among many other things a "Romeo e Giulietta" by Bellini's master, Niccolò Zingarelli, one of whose titles to fame was that he was Napoleon's favorite composer. In this Signorina Garcia, afterwards more famous as Mme. Malibran, took the part of Romeo, which, as in Bellini's opera, was written for a soprano. It was this libretto that, in accordance with a custom not then entirely obsolete, Bellini made use of, unchanged, for his own opera.

Richard Wagner wrote a Shakespearean opera, which had a single performance during his lifetime, in 1836, when he was twenty-three years old and director of a theatre in Magdeburg. It was "Das Liebesverbot," based upon "Measure for Measure," though in the libretto, which, like all his other librettos, he wrote himself, Shakespeare's play is very freely and somewhat "licentiously" treated. There was one disastrous performance then, which marked the end of Wagner's usefulness as operatic director at Magdeburg. In recent years the opera has been rescued from its long oblivion in the publication of the complete works of Wagner. He himself in later years spoke of its weakness; of the "reflection in it of modern French spirit," —that is, the reflection of the French spirit of 1836— "and, as concerns the melody, of Italian opera, upon my violently excited senses." Wagner called "Das Liebesverbot" a "youthful indiscretion"; and it was so indiscreet that it was not allowed to leave the archives of Wahnfried until very recent years.

"Macbeth" has attracted many ambitious composers; but not one has ever been able to make a musical setting of it that could long keep alive. The most significant is Verdi's, which he wrote in 1847 to a libretto of Francesco Piave, purveyor of texts for a number of his operas at that period, including "Rigoletto" and "La Traviata." Verdi rewrote the opera for performance in Paris in 1865. It had not been very successful before, though he cherished a special affection for it himself, and it has never had success in its new form. In his dedication of it to his son-in-law, Barezzi, he speaks of it as "My 'Macbeth,' which I love more than all my other works"—all the others, of course, that he had written up to that time. While the title-pages of the Italian editions bear the name of Piave as librettist, it is known that the scenario and the prose sketch of the work were the master's own; and that many of the verses are by the great Italian poet Maffei. The changes made for the Paris production of 1865, when Nuitter and Beaumont collaborated with the composer in preparing the new text, were radical. A revival of the opera in Stockholm in 1921 called renewed attention to what certain critics found to be germs of his later development, pointing as far forward as "Otello." Among other attempts at a "Macbeth" opera, that of the French composer, Chélard, in 1827, is notable only from the fact that the libretto was written by Rouget de l'Isle, who gained immortality as the author of the "Marseillaise."

Verdi's "Otello" seems to have had only one predecessor, also emanating from Italy, and enjoying a large measure of favor in its day. That was Rossini's. It was first produced in Naples in 1816, less than a year after "Il Barbiere di Siviglia." The principal soprano part was written for Mme. Colbran, whom Rossini afterwards married. The opera became greatly popular; and seemed at one time destined to outlive "Il Barbiere," which has celebrated its hundred and tenth birthday. It was considered to have "very dramatic music"; some compared it favorably, in part, at least, with "Don Giovanni" and "Fidelio." It differed — how much operas are apt to differ! — from Shakespeare. Iago is a quite subordinate character in it; Roderigo a prominent one. The instrumentation was thought to be shockingly noisy when the opera was new. It was one of the works in the new style by which the orchestra replaced the harpsichord or pianoforte in accompanying the recitatives. Garcia produced it in his New York season of 1825–26, when he took the part of Otello, and his daughter Maria — afterwards Mme. Malibran — that of Desdemona. Ireland, in his "Records of the New York Stage," reports contemporaneous whispers that "the fervency of the Signorina's acting and singing in this opera was attributable to her father's threat at rehearsal, where she had failed to throw sufficient spirit into her character, that if she did not improve in her rendition at night, he would, as Otello, not theatrically but really stab her to the heart, that being the mode in which the Italian Desdemona is despatched, instead of being smothered, as on the English stage." Allowing for some exaggeration, the story may be believed by those who know the other story of a passer-by in the street where Garcia lived. Startled by cries and screams, apparently of agony, and inquiring as to the cause, he was reassured by a neighbor, who said it was only Manuel Garcia giving his children a singing lesson.

Garcia, no doubt, brought some shocks to the easy-going dramatic standards of the time, which are illustrated by the anecdote of a listener whom the dênouement of "Otello" caused to cry out in excitement, "Good God! the tenor is murdering the soprano!"—something that was n't done.

"The Merry Wives of Windsor" has appealed strongly to constructors of opera in the comic vein, many of whom have attempted it. The liveliest of all "Falstaff's" predecessors is Otto Nicolai's "Merry Wives of Windsor," which can almost claim the title of a real Shakespearean opera, though its freshness and vigor have somewhat faded now. It may be doubted whether Hermann Goetz was quite the man to undertake an opera on "The Taming of the Shrew," which for a time seemed to many to deserve a place among the Shakespeareans. The man himself, something of a valetudinarian, had not a great sense of humor, and what he had was tinged with Teutonism. The music of his opera has a bit too much of German romanticism and not enough of the boisterous, ravaging farcicality of Shakespeare. The title of another "Shrew" setting is preserved, "La Capricciosa Corretta," composed in 1785 by Martin y Soler, once considered a rival of Mozart, a snatch of whose opera, "Una Cosa Rara," is quoted in the last act of "Don Giovanni" as the Don sits at the table. The chief point of interest in his Shakespearean opera is that the libretto is by Lorenzo da Ponte, who tasted of immortality through the librettos he wrote for Mozart, and who lived his last years, died, and was buried in New York.

A certain interest attaches to Hector Berlioz's one Shakespearean opera, "Béatrice et Bénédict," based, of course, on "Much Ado About Nothing," though it is a very free adaptation of Shakespeare's work. Berlioz was one of the few Frenchmen of his time who really loved and admired Shakespeare. Shakespeare was, indeed, one of his passions; and to be one of Berlioz's passions meant something. He himself arranged the libretto, in which, notwithstanding all his reverence for Shakespeare, he reduced all the subordinate characters to mere "feeders" for the two principals, and introduced a new one, intended to burlesque his redoubtable enemy, Fétis. But the opera has made very little stir upon the musical waters, even in the great patriotic Berlioz cult that arose in France after 1871. Sir Charles Stanford added to the Shakespearean list a "Much Ado About Nothing" that was produced at Covent Garden some years ago, and seems to have made little mark. As for "The Tempest," at least twenty operas

[145]

upon its subject might be enumerated, including efforts by Arne and by Halévy (composer of "La Juive"), all of which are dead, safely buried, and forgotten. How thoroughly an opera may pass out of the minds of men is shown not only by this list, but also by the fate of a "Winter's Tale" that Flotow wrote, and of a "Hermione" that Max Bruch produced upon the same subject; of the "Richard II's" and "Richard III's" of various composers; of the seven or eight operas more or less on Shakespearean subjects, much perverted, by Sir Henry Bishop; and much incidental music to the plays, from the earliest days to the present, from Purcell and Arne to Sullivan, Stanford, and later composers.

The orchestral works—overtures, tone poems and other symphonic illustrations of Shakespeare that have had a more or less prominent place in modern music—are almost innumerable. Among the most familiar are Tchaikovsky's "Romeo and Juliet" and "Hamlet" overtures (also his incidental music to "Hamlet"), and his "Tempest" fantasia; Berlioz's "King Lear" overture and his elaborate "Romeo and Juliet" symphony, with solos and choruses; Liszt's symphonic poem, "Hamlet"; Dvořák's "Othello" overture; Svendsen's "Romeo and Juliet" overture; Elgar's "Falstaff," Joachim's "Hamlet" overture; MacDowell's symphonic poems, "Hamlet" and "Ophelia"; Strauss's symphonic poem on "Macbeth," Weingartner's on "King Lear," Coleridge-Taylor's on "Othello." As a curiosity it might be mentioned that "William Shakespeare" wrote an orchestral overture called "After Seeing Rossi Play Hamlet"—William Shakespeare being the well-known English singing teacher of recent years.

THE MODERNIZING OF BACH

THERE is always the occasion for discussion and dispute as to the proper performance at the present time of music of the eighteenth century and earlier. The great change that came about at the beginning of the nineteenth century, not only in the spirit of music but as well in the means of its performance, resulted in the rapid obsolescence of the old ways, even in a speedy forgetfulness of many of them. It is only in recent years, when there has been a revival of interest in the old music, that there has also come the study of the old methods and an attempt to understand just how the old music was performed, as an aid in penetrating into its spirit and in reproducing it.

The greatest of the eighteenth century composers — and the qualification is not to be limited to the eighteenth century — was Johann Sebastian Bach. With the great revival of interest in his work that began with Mendelssohn's performance of the "Matthew Passion" in 1829 and that later led to the publication of a complete edition of his works, begun in 1850 and not finished till fifty years later, came the realization that it was not so easy as it at first seemed to recreate the work of Bach for the public of the present day. Bach wrote for the public

The Modernizing of Bach

of his time. He stood at the confines of the modern world, but never crossed them, so far as concerns the means and apparatus he employed.

Reflections such as these are aroused by certain valiant attempts at the performance of Bach's music for modern listeners. There was Leopold Stokowski, conductor of the Philadelphia Orchestra, who played Bach's six Brandenburg Concertos, in their numerical order, in two concerts—an arduous undertaking. There was Harold Samuel, the English pianist, who gave in New York, as he had frequently done in London, six pianoforte recitals on six successive days, devoted entirely to the clavier music of Bach,—in some ways a still more arduous undertaking. We need not discuss now the artistic justification of playing so much of Bach's music at once, in concerts devoted exclusively to that music.

Mr. Stokowski made a brave effort—in certain directions—to overcome difficulties that Bach planted in the way of modern performances: technical difficulties in the playing of certain instruments, the difficulty or impossibility of obtaining certain others. Quite insuperable were such difficulties as using an orchestra of the size Bach had at his disposal, in a room of the size that Bach used;

and, it might be added, the provision of eighteenth century ears, minds, and attitude toward music.

There has been criticism of Mr. Samuel's proceedings also. There has been criticism of the spirit in which he played the music. There has been other criticism, perhaps more cogent, of the instrument he used. Bach, of course, wrote for the harpsichord, and presumably used, in the privacy of his own home, the clavichord, which could hardly be heard across a room of ordinary size. There has been dispute of a statement of one of his old biographers that the clavichord was his "favorite instrument." There was no clavichord among his possessions at the time of his death, though he left several harpsichords. But so far as relates to public performances to-day, that matter is purely academic. Only the harpsichord can be in question, and there may be more in that than meets the eye.

Mr. Samuel's performances were the subject of public correspondence. One writer, speaking of them especially, though his remarks might have applied to other performances of Bach's clavier works on the pianoforte, after praising Mr. Samuel's excellent work and admiring the "devotion" of the audience, declared that the "young people among the

The Modernizing of Bach

listeners ought to be told the whole truth." In his
view, the whole truth was this:

The pianoforte translation of Bach's clavier works
is a complete misrepresentation of the original; and
if J. S. Bach had stalked into Town Hall he would
have shot Samuel on the spot. For he was almost
as much of a virtuoso as he was a mystic, and to
hear his flaming music stripped of its color and mul-
titudinous glory and reduced to a two-voiced drab-
ness would have moved him to wrath and perhaps
tears, too, if he had known that these young people
were reverently accepting that sound as the true
Bach. They ought to know that the harpsichord is
a diatonic instrument, while the pianoforte is "ar-
peggiotic" [which he emphasizes as a "good word"],
so that, with no chance to use the pedal, naturally
the modern instrument is suffocated and not at its
best, even when translating — that they are getting
only the spiritual and intellectual part of a crea-
ture that is magnificently sensuous — that at most
they are being impressed by a part only, like the
visible peak of a floating iceberg.

When all this is made clear to them, they will
be in a way to conceive the incredible vitality of
this music which, after being buried for a hundred
years and then resurrected into a world speaking

another language, dismembered and stunted, with all its color gone, still moves them as nothing else can.

Well, even granting all this, what is to be done? Much thought on the subject will bring perhaps different conclusions at different times. Some may think there is no universally valid conclusion. The gloomier pessimists may think that the only way to avoid displeasing the returning spirit of Bach and to avoid getting shot is to make a Bach-less world. But is it certain that this would please the returning spirit?

The splendors of the harpsichord, not equally relished by all music lovers, were first revealed to this modern public some twenty-five years ago when Arnold Dolmetsch first gave his concerts in New York. Since then there have been some, as Messrs. Whiting and Richards and others, who have labored as in a missionary field. There has been the admirable English player, Mrs. Woodhouse, and the distinguished champion, Mme. Landowska. There are difficulties in the way of the evangel. There have to be modern harpsichords that "carry" in modern halls —larger than the ancient ones—better than the old instruments. Now, too, Mr. Dolmetsch has invented a harpsichord on which accents, crescendos,

The Modernizing of Bach

and diminuendos can be made, quite impossible on the old instrument and hence not reckoned with in the music that was written for it.

Would these things satisfy the returning spirit of Bach? If not, and if an old harpsichord must be used, there must be a concert room as small as those at Bach's disposal. If the player is going to earn his living, prices must be raised to correspond. So there would be no danger of many of the correspondent's "devoted young people" getting wrong impressions: they would not be able to go, and would get no impressions at all.

If Bach came back to hear his music played on a modern organ, he would be in the way of hearing something he never heard before. Whether his impulsive temperament would lead him again to shoot at sight must be left to the correspondent. Sir Charles Stanford, the British composer, as a young man, examined Bach's organ in the Thomaskirche in Leipsic, when it was, he believed, practically in the same state as it was in Bach's time. In his book, "Pages From an Unwritten Diary," he says: "To an English ear it seemed all reeds and manual mixtures. The mechanism was truly horrible, the keys almost needed a Nasmyth hammer to depress them; and the pedals were so broad and clumsy that it

was a matter of luck to put down the right note."
The tempos and registration of even the most skilful and reverential modern organist do not reproduce, for us, the effects of such an organ.

The size and proportions of Bach's orchestra are
well known. They are not in the remotest degree
like ours, and the playing of his orchestral pieces
could not have borne any resemblance to our playing of them. The very violins were a different instrument, with their loosely haired, stiff, old-fash-
ioned bows, their short necks, and their tuning to
a pitch a tone or a tone and a half lower than ours,
the sound being correspondingly less brilliant. Nor
is there need to mention the trumpets and horns,
with two classes of players for the high and low
ranges respectively, and the high range so high as
to be appalling to our players, used in large measure,
probably, in order to get even a partially complete
scale, though with certain of the notes definitely
and irrevocably out of tune and the rest shrill and
shrieking. Nor need the obsolete instruments be
more than mentioned, by which Bach set such store:
the viola da gamba—which must have given the
sixth "Brandenburg" concerto a wholly different
sound from what it has in a modern orchestra's
performance, to say nothing of the fact that it is

The Modernizing of Bach

on the border line of chamber music. There are the "violino piccolo" (which Bach used in the first "Brandenburg" concerto and present-day conductors very naturally do not); the "viola pomposa," Bach's own invention; the "viola d'amore"—gigantic efforts in recent years have resulted in hearing the viola d'amore in some of its proper places on rare occasions; but the addresses of three or four viola da gamba players are not known in New York. Or there are the "oboe d'amore" and the "oboe da caccia," for which Bach calculated some special effects; or the "flûte à bec" (the flageolet), or the "cornetto," a wood-wind instrument, not the brass one of modern times. There are others. Many of these cannot be reproduced in effect to-day except approximately. Bach would have a good deal of shooting to do, once he got going.

Or there might be deliberation about the singers. Were there any in Bach's day who could sing his solo airs any better than the best singers to-day? Many of these airs seem to us quite unvocal and can be sung only with great labor and frequent signs of distress. Did Bach ever have singers who could make them sound natural? As for his chorus of a dozen or a dozen and a half singers, was he fixed in his liking for that number? He was undoubtedly sternly limited to it. His orchestra was of about the same size. Both he and Handel (who had command of larger resources) expected their orchestras to be about as numerous as their choruses. What would Bach say to a chorus of 200 or 300 and an orchestra of only 80 or 90, which we use to present his choral works to-day?

Bach was a great experimenter in tone color; but we can reproduce his experiments to-day only within narrow limits. It is very well to say, Bach would have liked this modern thing or would have hated that. It all depends on the sentiment, fancy, tastes, likes, or dislikes of whoever says it. Robert Franz, some sixty years ago, when he made his arrangements of cantatas by Bach and of arias by Bach and Handel, roused a great controversy by his liberties. They do not all seem destructive now. It does not seem certain that we are authorized to say what Bach would have liked or what he would n't. He did not like the Silbermann pianofortes that Frederick the Great showed him on his visit to Potsdam in 1747; but the Silbermann pianofortes were not Steinways; and one man's guess as to what he would have thought of Steinways is as good as another's.

So it seems almost as if we must have either a Bach-less world or a compromise. There may be

The Modernizing of Bach

room for a difference of opinion as to the playing of the harpsichord pieces on the modern piano. Some, as Messrs. Arthur Whiting and Harold Bauer, have made arrangements of them for the piano in which the use of certain eight-foot and four-foot stops of the harpsichord may be represented by octave doublings and by a change of the relative positions of certain voices; but this cannot be done with pieces in the stricter forms (as canon and fugue), and gives hardly more than a hint of the harpsichord. The playing of the clavier pieces, as they appear on Bach's printed page, on the piano, by Mr. Samuel and by other sympathetic interpreters does not, to many people, seem dry — evidently. The effect is not that of the harpsichord any more than the effect of almost everything else we perform of Bach is as he wrote it. But effect does not seem to be lacking.

These things being so, or not being so, the question arises, is it possible at this age of the world to give Bach's music without more or less "modernizing" it; if not, how far is it justifiable to go in "modernizing"? — and if no modernizing is permissible, whether the only alternative is a Bach-less world. It may be said that the ears, minds, and souls of the twentieth century, being what they are, cannot hear this music of the early eighteenth century as its contemporaries heard it. The ears, minds, and souls of our ancestors for the last 200 years have been undergoing change, and ours are the result of it — call it development, advance, or, as some champions of the old call it, retrogression and deterioration. Whatever it is, it is change. Even if a concert of Bach's music were given now in physical conditions and surroundings exactly as it was given in Bach's day, we should not hear it as his contemporaries heard it. If we cannot have the old harpsichord, should we use the pianoforte? If our organ is a different affair from Bach's, should we use ours, or give up the organ? If we cannot profitably or in any other way provide an orchestra of Bach's size to play his music, may we use ours? If we no longer have the obsolete instruments and their players, may we go on using substitutes — and where shall substitution stop? If we cannot have chorus and orchestra balanced as in Bach's day, shall we continue to use our own balance?

All these things "modernize" and hence, in so far, destroy the effects Bach heard and counted on hearing. If he comes back to shoot, why should he select any one class of performers to be his target rather than any other? Can any say confidently, Bach would have liked this, so we will do it; and Bach

The Modernizing of Bach

wouldn't have liked that, so we mustn't do it? Suppose somebody else, also musical in feeling and, so far as may be, "authoritative," says something else—who shall decide between the disagreeing doctors? We are thrown into a sea of doubt and conjecture.

If he has any shooting to do, many will think that Bach will reserve his aim for those who thunder transcriptions of his organ pieces on the pianoforte, solely to make a holiday for those virtuosos who find his harpsichord works insufficient for the display of their strength and facility; and perhaps especially for those who pound that much-distorted version of the "Chaconne" for violin solo in D minor. How much he will reserve for those who transfer to the modern orchestra the "thunder in his lifted hand" which Bach bestowed upon the organ and intended for the organ, may be left to conjecture.

USURPATIONS OF THE BALLET

THE needs of the new art of the Russian ballet which has been so zealously exploited in Paris, London, New York, and Chicago take it far beyond music hitherto specially provided for it. It now claims the whole art of music for its field. The eagerness of promoters in laying hold of anything and everything they think can be applied and exploited is something that arouses questioning and even resentment in the minds of many music-lovers. The promoters and exploiters go farther, and announce that music is not an art capable of standing by itself, but needs the ballet-dancer to complete and interpret it. The art of the ballet-dancer, we are told, "glimpses the secret of music, envisaged in forms of line, movement, color and rhythm." It "suggests what music alone of all the arts possesses — complete freedom from the things of the earth and the material boundaries of existence. Revelations, so made by physical means, are of the incorporeal and the realm that lies beyond good and evil. At the same time its motives come from life and nature, from other arts and from the most varied fields of human experience." All this is called forth by the art of Mme. Pawlowa, and her pleasing contortions to music. The general proposition is that music is not in itself com-

Usurpations of the Ballet

plete, an art capable of standing by itself, but needs the ballet-dancer to complement, to perfect, and to interpret it. A more special application of this great theorem is made to the works of American composers. Before they can write "interesting" music there must be "an internal revolution in the breast of the composer, a vast liberation from provincialism and self-consciousness and a vivid perception of beauty that pervades life and informs joyous, living art."

And how is this revolution, this liberation, this perception to be accomplished? Why, by nothing other than the proceedings of the ballet-dancer, especially by those of the charming Pawlowa. Nobody will doubt the beneficent effects of liberation and perception, if and when they are effected. But they will not be produced by the dancers whose pretensions have been so hugely increased in recent years. There is nothing, really, against the ballet-dancers. Their art is a very pretty one when it is prettily exercised, and forms a pleasant diversion for those who like this sort of thing. The more philosophical observers, if they can disengage their minds for a moment from the present fascinations of the ballerina, may reflect that dancing has a highly respectable antiquity and is reputably connected with the first budding developments of musical art, how-

ever widely they have since parted company. They
have parted widely; and when the dancers come to
usurping a place in the present art of music, and
shoving and hustling that art about as they have
been doing, there is need of a deep diapason of
protest.

There is need of protest against the idea that the
ballet-dancers can in some way interpret or illumine
or give some real significance to music that it did
not have before; to music that the innocent composer thought was in itself and with no outside aid,
expressing all he had in him to say or to express,
and who never dreamed of the need of its being
"mimed." This dancing that its admirers think has
acquired so many disciples and has become such
an important part of artistic life, is a damnable
perversion of the art of great masters, when the
dancers lay violent hands — or feet — upon it and
force it into their own service. When one of them
"danced" Beethoven's Seventh Symphony, she
calmly announced that she was "interpreting" it,
as if Beethoven himself had not done all the interpreting of his own ideas that was necessary or possible when he put them down upon paper and gave
the score to the world to play as he wrote it. There
was a miserable performance by a band of scratch

players and a woman in tights and cheese-cloth
draperies writhing on the stage, and the symphony
was "interpreted," as no mere musician had ever
interpreted it. The dancer was led to it, no doubt,
by Wagner's foolish remarks about the Seventh
Symphony being the " apotheosis of the dance " —
remarks which he probably would hastily have
withdrawn if he could have foreseen the results.
Beethoven himself never gave any hint that he considered his symphony anything of the kind; and
nobody could by any possibility have gained anything but a wrong, distorted, cheapened, vulgarized
idea of Beethoven's work, and what he intended by
it, from any such performance. But now no such excuse as a Wagnerian essay is needed for the appropriation of a masterpiece; every dancer takes her
own wherever she finds it. There is the " Carnaval "
of Schumann — like Walther von der Vogelweide,
in Beckmesser's terms, " ein guter Meister, doch
lang schon todt," and consequently unable to help
himself by injunction or otherwise. He wrote it for
the pianoforte. It is as much of a pianoforte piece,
as little of an orchestral piece, as can well be imagined. It is a very epitome of Schumann's pianoforte style. Messrs. Rimsky Korsakoff, Glazunoff,
Liadow, and Tcherepnine conspired to transcribe it

for orchestra, for the purposes of " miming." They should all have been in better business. The transcription is not an effective orchestral piece; it misrepresents Schumann's thought and is only a makeshift for the purpose to which it has been turned. Some excuse has been made for dancing or "miming" the " Carnaval" on the ground that it suggests a ball and is, in part, composed of music more or less " dansante." But dancing it only implies a subtler form of the disintegration of taste and right understanding that is implied in all this making of masterpieces into ballet dances. Schumann's imagination, fancy, tenderness, passion, gayety, humor, are all contained completely in the music and are embodied in it conclusively for those who have ears to hear and imagination and intelligence to understand. To " dance " it puts it on the same plane as those picture newspapers for people too indolent or too ignorant to read.

Or there is Rimsky Korsakoff's "Scheherazade," which an avenging fate has also led the dancers to pervert to their uses. He thought he was writing in his orchestral composition an imaginative piece of programme music, not following an anecdote closely, but giving hints and suggestions and stimulating the imagination by his rich thematic in-

vention and glowing orchestration — about what?
Why, in the first movement, about the sea, which
is suggested in the broad sweep of the melodic line,
going perhaps as far as programme music can well
go in such an undertaking; and then about the
Kalandar Princes; and the young prince and the
young princess, whose likeness is suggested by the
resemblance of two themes; and then the festival
at Bagdad, the sea again, the shipwreck; and there is
a characteristic recurring theme representing Sche-
herezade, who relates these four wonderful stories.
But what becomes of all this carefully wrought
musical picturing when the piece is "mimed" by a
ballet? The music is there; its substance and
quality are not changed — but, lo! everything else
is changed. Its "meaning" has been overturned
without a word. We are now invited to see in it,
or at least through it, the depiction of King Shah-
riar's discovery of the faithlessness of his favorite,
his surprise of her and the other women of his harem
in the arms of their lovers — all cut down and slain
except the princess, who snatches the executioner's
sword and kills herself. What has become of the salt
smell of the sea that the confirmed programme
musicians have found in the original? The poor
composer is nothing so long as the popular and

brilliant dancer can make use of him in her way.

So, too, those who have glimpsed with Debussy the delicious figure of his faun and his bewildered reveries by the wood, on the shore of the lake, will not thank the Russian dancers for the opportunity that it occurred neither to Mallarmé nor to Debussy to present, of seeing a nymph drop her nether garment. Nor will they find the suggestion of lust, however veiled, at home in the charm of Debussy's music.

The favorite Russian dancers may be, and very possibly are, all that their fervent admirers paint them, in their own art; though some may think that there are or have been in any art very few practitioners, living or dead, who can or could have lived up to some of the praise that has been bestowed on these estimable ladies and gentlemen. There are many who cannot understand or appreciate their art on any such standard, and who cannot realize that they have made any such revelation of a new heaven or a new earth as has been described. But when their tribe come shouldering their way into the art of music with the pretension of widening its boundaries, or increasing its potentialities, or giving it "freedom," or teaching it anything whatever; or when their devotees undertake to show

Usurpations of the Ballet

that the "scale practice" or the "harmony grammars" of the mere musicians are small and useless things—as they have undertaken to show—compared with the muscular exercises, leaps, and contortions, however graceful, that utilize the musical material to which scales and harmonic knowledge are indispensable; or characterize as " mere bookworms" the followers of music who refuse to be seduced by the contortionists — then these worms ("bookworms," no doubt) turn, and wish to scratch, so far as worms can scratch.

Admirable, graceful, agreeable, and thoroughly developed in muscle as these Russian and other dancers are, they are humble and not quite necessary appendages to the art of music, which is not beholden to them for any instruction, illumination or liberation whatever.

SCHUMANN'S CHILDREN

ROBERT and Clara Schumann, whose marriage in 1840 was the culmination of a romantic struggle of several years' duration, as all readers of the composer's biography know, had eight children, of whom seven lived to grow up. They do not cut much figure in the biographies of the master; but readers of the biography and letters of Frau Clara Schumann, and especially of the recently published correspondence between her and Johannes Brahms, will realize how deeply these children affected the life of their mother. They will see how the fate of several of them intensified the tragic aureole that surrounded Frau Clara, who survived her husband so many years and had to suffer many things from which death had released him. She had much to bear in the mental collapse and premature death of her husband and later still more in the sadly tangled and suddenly snapped strands of her children's destinies.

It is a fact, lamentable from some points of view, from others perhaps a beneficent safeguard from the arrogance of dynasties, that genius — musical genius no more than any other — is not inherited. It is one of nature's incommunicable mysteries. There is the Bach family to make a glowing but almost solitary exception. There are Alessandro Scarlatti, the father, and Domenico Scarlatti, the son, both geniuses of a secondary order, to make a somewhat less notable one. How many others can a survey of musical history show? Robert Schumann had no musical genius among his ancestors; he left none among his descendants. But he inherited a mental instability that remained with him all his life, making itself now and again alarmingly felt, even in his earlier years, and apparently affecting his character and his intellectual life more or less till the end. He died in an insane asylum after a couple of years' struggle with insanity, during which he tried to take his own life. The particular form of his malady seems, to physicians of the present day who have studied reports of the case, to have been what is called "dementia praecox." Unfortunately, if genius is not inherited, mental instability is; and so, some of Schumann's children had a physical and mental inheritance that would make a modern pathologist shake his head.

As readers of the Schumann biography will remember, and as some will know from personal knowledge, Clara Schumann was a pianist when she married in 1840, and kept up her career as a solo performer, in which she became one of the most distinguished and most admired of her time, till nearly the end of her life. She died in 1896, at the age of 77. Her children, during this career as a virtuoso, were alternately a blessing and a burden to her, and the lot of several of them a source of inextinguishable grief.

They were: Marie, born in 1841; Elise, in 1843; Julie, in 1845; Ludwig, in 1848; Ferdinand, in 1848; Ferdinand, in 1849; Eugenie, in 1851, and Felix, in 1854.

The three sons caused the mother the greatest anxiety. It is clear enough now that upon them chiefly descended the "bad inheritance" from their father, physically and mentally. When he died in 1856, Ludwig was 8 years old, Ferdinand was 7, and Felix, who never saw his father, 2. They were all separated when the time came for them to go to school. Clara Schumann was constantly away on concert tours and quite unable to give them such a family life as she would have liked to. Ludwig and Ferdinand were sent away to school, first together to Berlin; then they had to be separated. Ludwig in 1861 was placed in Karlsruhe. His physician and his teacher advised the mother that his health was not such that he could remain in a public school, but should be sent to the country. When Ludwig's schooling was finished, he was put into the book trade, in Karlsruhe, to follow in his grandfather

Schumann's footsteps. But he had no taste for it and wished for something else. His lack of concentration and singleness of purpose caused his mother great anxiety. She wrote to a friend in 1865:

"I cannot tell you what anxiety such a young man can cause! Imagine a dreamy youth who has no special taste for anything but dreaming, who is so unpractical from every point of view that even his teachers say they have not the slightest idea what to do with him. And now I must choose his career for him! How many sleepless nights has this cost me! I should like to give him a higher intellectual training; but the time has come when he must enter practical life, otherwise he is lost."

He went into a music dealer's shop in Leipsic, but could not keep his place. He was hard to get along with and changed his positions frequently. His relations with his family were unsatisfactory in his adolescent days and his mother at times got quite out of patience with him. Finally, in 1868, her friend Raymond Härtel, the music publisher of Leipsic, was obliged to tell her that Ludwig's mind was disordered; the sad intelligence was confirmed in the next few weeks from several other quarters. He was taken for a time to his grandfather Wieck's, then to Baden. His mother reports him in 1869 as "studying" — he wished to become a musician, much against her will; but his condition changed her attitude toward him and made her let him have freer play for his inclinations. He advertised himself as a teacher in Dresden and even hoped to give concerts. But it became clear that he had neither ear nor rhythmic sense; he attempted composition, but the results were so extremely bad that his mother was again much disturbed. The conclusion finally became unavoidable that he was incurably insane. He had to be put into an asylum; going from one to another, he steadily became worse, till he died in 1879.

Ferdinand, the next to the youngest of the children, born in 1849, was "a reasonably satisfactory child." He acquitted himself creditably at school, and in 1866 was put into business; through the influence of the Mendelssohn family in Berlin he got a place in an important business house in that city and did well there. In the Franco-Prussian war he served in the army and returned unscathed. Very soon thereafter he surprised and distressed his mother with the news of his engagement to a Fräulein Antonia Deutsch — she regarded him as much too young and his position too little established to marry; but marry he did, and had several children.

Schumann's Children

Unfortunately, he became a victim of the morphine habit, whereby his health was entirely undermined. His struggles to free himself from the habit in one institution after another were in vain. He and his family became a burden upon his mother, adding still more to her anxieties. He died after a long and depressing illness in 1891 — his death being a release for himself and for his mother, yet for her one more deep grief. He left another burden behind — his eldest son, also Ferdinand, had to be put into some business. It was decided that he should become a druggist; and after much trouble he was suitably apprenticed. But he found he did not like the trade. He, too, wished to be a musician. His grandmother found him of "a dreamy nature, such as becomes a musician more than a tradesman." She thought he might make himself a good teacher; he had "decided talent," but it was too late for him to become a pianist. Perhaps he might, she thought, make a good position for himself as a teacher in America or England — the compliment will not be appreciated in either country — but not in Germany. Here was another distracting problem falling to the poor woman to solve.

"This leaves me only one son," wrote Mme. Schumann sadly to Joachim, announcing to him the death of Ferdinand, "whom we can consider only as in a living death." This was Felix, the youngest child, and perhaps the greatest grief of all to the much-tried mother. As a boy at school he had, on the whole, made a poor showing, and some of his mother's letters to him — she hoped he would be a scholar — are full of reproaches. She was much distressed when, at the age of 13, he announced his strong desire to become a violinist. A touching letter from her is preserved in which she points out to him the heavy burden that would rest on him as the son of Robert Schumann if he appeared as a musician. She wrote, in 1867, thus:

"Your grandmother and Ferdinand write me that you are going about with the idea of becoming a violinist. That would be a grave step, more serious than you can realize. If you are not a distinguished violinist, no matter how clever you are, you will have a burdensome part to play as the son of Robert Schumann. As I say, you can live up to your name only if you develop really important genius as a musician; and, thus endowed, study with enormous industry. Fully as I am convinced that, with your talent, you can give yourself and others pleasure as an amateur (though even that will require hard work), I do not at all believe that you have such a

gift as is required for high artistic rank." Joachim
was called in to decide; and in accordance with his
decision it was determined that Felix should finish
his high-school course and not pay too much attention to music, especially as his constitution appeared
to be not of the strongest. He went on with school
and then entered Heidelberg University.

Felix did develop, however, considerable talent
as a poet. This was shown in various productions
he contributed to home festivals at Christmastide
and on other occasions. And he tasted of immortality through the fact that three of his poems were
chosen by Brahms for songs — one of them being
among the finest and most popular of his compositions, "Meine Lieb' ist grün." This, and the one next
following it in the "Lieder und Gesänge," Op. 63
(Nos. 5 and 6, grouped together as "Junge Lieder")
are marked in the original editions with the initials
"F. S." only. The second is less well known. The
song entitled "Versunken," No. 5 in Op. 86, is signed
with Felix Schumann's name in full. When Brahms
composed "Meine Lieb' ist grün" in 1874—the
young poet was then twenty years old—he sent it
on to Frau Schumann in Berlin, who thus describes
the occasion in a letter to Brahms:

"The song was a delightful surprise and especially

so for Felix, whom we had not told about it. When Joachim came in the evening I showed it to him, we began to play it, and Felix came up and asked what words they were. When he saw his own, he became quite pale!"

In that year it was discovered that the young man's lungs were attacked; and a new source of anxiety and sorrow came into his mother's life. He had to be sent to Davos in the summer. She writes to Brahms:

"Can you imagine the feelings of a mother who has one son in a living grave; another, so richly endowed by nature, living with her, sick, with very little hope of saving him; or, if she does, with the prospect of never seeing him completely well again; a dear child, also richly endowed, dead and buried as she was in the very midst of her happiness"—this was her daughter Julie, who married in Italy and died there after three years of married life—"If you can put yourself in my place, you will surely not think less well of me if now and again I let my sorrow overflow into the heart of a sympathizing friend." Nobly and tenderly did Brahms appreciate her feelings and respond to them.

Felix remained in Switzerland for the climate; and in Zurich took up the study of philology and modern languages instead of the law, towards which he had been looking in the university, but for which his mother was sure he had no talent. The poor lady was again troubled because he wished to publish certain literary efforts; she wrote him that he must do so anonymously at first, so that he and his family might be spared disagreeable comment in case they were not well received; for, with his name, more would be expected of him than of another. This, she wrote to Brahms, seemed to irritate him extremely; and he sent her letters so unkind, so unloving, that she was much distressed. She implores Brahms, if he sees Felix, to try to win some influence over him, to show him that his views on life are quite unsound and bring him to a realization of the duties he owed his family — certainly no slight commission even for a devoted friend.

Then Felix lived in Italy a year or so. By 1878 his condition was much worse and he was brought back to Germany, where he lingered a year and died in February, 1879, twenty-five years old.

Of the four daughters, Marie, the eldest child, born in 1841, passed much of her life as the companion and helper of her mother, often accompanying her on her numerous concert tours. It is obvious that under such circumstances any keeping up of her own musicianship was out of the question.

Musical Discourse

Eugenie, the sixth child who grew up, and the fourth daughter, was born in 1851. She never gained a very conspicuous place in her art, but her mother at one time had some expectations of her as a pianist and expressed the hope that the Schumann tradition might be handed down through her. She wrote in her diary in 1882, at Frankfort:

"I have Marie and Eugenie play for me on Sundays. It is wrong for me not to take pains with them when they play so nicely, and have such a subtle understanding. I have no other such pupils as these two. I am troubled that I am always a hindrance to them. Nobody knows what they can do, as they never play when I am by."

In 1895 she wrote: "Eugenie played for me several times. Every time I hear her I find her a riper artist; if only she were not so physically frail!" Joachim played with her a few times in London on semi-public occasions—more, no doubt, because of his intimate friendship with her parents than because of her specific abilities—but her life in London, where she lived for many years, was spent mostly in the drudgery of teaching. In later years Marie and Eugenie lived in Switzerland, two old ladies much reduced in circumstances by the war.

Julie, the third daughter, was also a source of

anxiety to her mother on account of her health. In 1868, when she was twenty-three years old, she was sent to Divonne, a French health resort. There she met Count Radicati di Marmorito, an Italian of good family, to whom she lost her heart, and they became engaged after an acquaintance of seven weeks, though a formal betrothal did not take place till later. Frau Schumann—who cannot be blamed, in her long life of trials and griefs, for taking some things harder than may seem absolutely necessary —was distressed. Marmorito was an Italian and a Catholic. She could hardly speak a word to him, she says in one of her letters, because of the barrier of language. Nor was the Count's family favorably disposed to the match. But difficulties and objections were overcome, and they were married in 1869. He seems to have been a devoted husband, and a help to his mother-in-law in some of her later trials. From this happy outcome now arose suddenly a new occasion for perplexity and unhappiness on the part of the mother. Ever since his first acquaintance with Robert Schumann, Johannes Brahms had been an intimate friend of the Schumann family, and especially since Robert Schumann's death he had been a help and a dependence for the widow. When the news of Julie's engagement arrived, he suddenly became gloomy and silent. Max Kalbeck, in his life of Brahms, says that there is nothing in the suggestion that Brahms was hard hit by Julie Schumann's engagement to the Italian Count. But Clara Schumann thought differently. She wrote to a friend thus:

"Johannes, from the moment that I told him the news of Julie's engagement, was entirely changed; he overcame it in a fortnight or so, but he hardly says a thing to Julie, though formerly he had many words and glances for her. Levi told me a few days ago that Brahms was head over ears in love with Julie." In her diary she wrote: "Johannes is a changed man now; he comes rarely to us and speaks in monosyllables, even to Julie towards whom he was formerly always so amiable. Has he really been in love with her? But he never thought of marriage and Julie never had any tender feeling for him." Brahms was the elder by thirteen years. If there was anything in this, it was soon over.

Julie's happiness in her Italy was short. She died in November, 1872, after little more than three years of married life, leaving Count Marmorito with two boys, and causing one more sorrow to her much-tried mother. In 1877 a grandson, the elder boy, Robert, a gifted lad, dear to Clara, also died.

Schumann's Children

There was one more child, of Robert and Clara Schumann, a daughter, Elise, born in 1843, who took up the study of the pianoforte and began teaching in Frankfort. She made a début in that city with her mother and Joachim, in 1865—according to the mother's report to Brahms, a brilliant occasion. Mother and daughter played together Schumann's "Andante and Variations" for two pianofortes, Op. 46; everything went "wunderschön" and brought forth immense applause. But the career of a German Hausfrau, and not that of a pianist, was the destiny of Elise. In 1877 she married Louis Sommerhoff, whom Frau Clara reported to be "a very charming, excellent man from America. He is a merchant, well situated there, and hopes in a few years to be able to return to Europe." And this he apparently did.

Of the scandalous charges recently made public by one of Schumann's grandchildren, involving wrong-doing on the part of Frau Clara and Brahms in the early years of their friendship, and the illegitimacy of the youngest Schumann child, there is surely no need to speak at length. Clara's devotion to the memory of her husband, the austerity of her character and of her whole life, Brahms's reverence for one whom he regarded as his master, the tenderness of the friendship between him and that master's widow, all stand as witnesses against the falsehood. Some have tried to find in this charge ground for the destruction of some of the earlier letters between the two in the correspondence recently published in Germany. But character, tested and proved, still counts for something in the minds of decent and sensible people.

BERLIOZ TO-DAY

IT is still the fashion with some of Berlioz's advocates to declare that the world has not yet given him a real chance; and they are pertinaciously saying that he will yet win his way to universal acceptance. Perhaps the warmth has somewhat faded from these claims since they got a fillip from the hundredth anniversary of Berlioz's birth, in 1903. For there has been no lack of opportunity to become converted to admiration and love of his music. But the public for the greater part remains cold, listens to it as a duty, and returns to most of it—there are a few exceptions—with reluctance. The musical public of New York has become familiar with the works of the French composer, with the important exception of the operas, since that concert by the Philharmonic Society in 1846, when his overture, "Les Francs Juges," was played, the first of his compositions to be heard in the New World.

Berlioz himself loudly bewailed the neglect with which he was treated. But if any ambitious genius ever has had a chance, it has been Berlioz. His works were not entirely hidden under a bushel in Paris during his lifetime; and within the last fifty-odd years—after the Franco-Prussian war, to connect the cause with the effect—there was organized and sustained effort in France to make a national, a patriotic duty of performing them, of hearing them, of admiring them, as an offset to the Teutonic influences that for a time threatened to overwhelm the art of music in France, and for a time did so. In Germany, from his earlier days, Berlioz found an abundant hearing and a welcome in person and for his music. He was received with deference and admiration in England, though it would have been expecting too much to find his music warmly welcomed there in the middle of the last century. The musical records of New York and Boston show how long his name and his music have been familiar in those cities.

So it is by no means true, as has been maintained, that Berlioz has been anywhere " practically avoided." His music has been presented abundantly, zealously, by conductors and artists who have identified themselves as completely as might be with his spirit. But, as years have gone by, it has become increasingly evident that but little of this music, and that of comparatively small significance in the whole mass of his work, has made good a claim upon the love and sincere admiration of the public. Presented as the fairest product of the modern impulse of its time in art, it somehow turns to ashes like Dead Sea fruit, as you try to lay hold of it.

Berlioz To-day

And yet, while the music of Berlioz has thus failed, and is every day failing, to impress itself as a living reality, volumes have been written and discussions have filled the musical world about Berlioz the man, the musician, the pioneer, the great composer, the discoverer of the mighty fabric of a new and immortal art, the originator of the modern orchestra, the one who turned the attention of a waiting world to all the promise and potency of programme music, a creator of deathless fame; or the poseur, the charlatan, the huckster of musical claptrap, the impotent striver after great things, the architect of great imaginings that collapsed like card houses, the schemer of musical magnificences whose creative power panted in vain after his ambition. There is something puissant about the man, his personality, his career, and some aspects of his achievements to account for all this. It is not the legacy of a nobody. But the earnest seeker will have to find it elsewhere than in his music, which many people talk about, but few love; and which, for the most part, falls so dead upon the imagination and sympathy of the listener.

In truth, the interesting things about Berlioz are literary, historical, technical, personal, psychological—almost anything but musical. It has been justly remarked that for many of the most enthusiastic appreciations of his music we must turn to the literary critics with a taste for music rather than to the musical public. Berlioz is a fascinating figure in a curiously engaging period. He came upon the scene in France in the midst of the welter of the romantic movement in literature and art—not unfortunately, as M. André Hallays has said, but rather, as it seems, fortunately, for the development of the essential qualities of the man and the musician. His personality projects itself vividly athwart that period in French art of " broken rules, abolished conventions, glorified passions," as one of the most insistent, violent, and volubly self-expressive personages in it. His life was a perpetual paroxysm of love, hate, grief, hyperbolic and unmeasurable emotion. He was, as Saint-Saëns called him, "paradox made man." It is impossible to take at all seriously the extravagant, the flamboyant portrait of himself and his experiences that Berlioz has left behind in his own writings—and as a writer he is equalled for voluminousness only by Wagner. Adolphe Boschot, his latest and best equipped biographer, has translated into sober truth the fantastic tales that Berlioz set down about himself — many of them something more than over-accentuations and exaggerations—and in quoting Berlioz's own description of these things, there is something very like a grin upon his biographer's face, ardent admirer and sympathizer though he is.

For thirty years Berlioz wrote the musical *feuilletons* of the *Journal des Débats*. As critic he was of piercing originality of view, intense conviction, and eccentric limitations. His attitude is always personal; and in his criticism he is as self-revealing as he is in his letters and his autobiography that complete the list of his published writings. If Berlioz's music can seldom engross and enchain the listener's interest, his prose style seldom fails to enchain and engross his reader's. Fate cast him into the vortex of Parisian journalism; but his writing had something in it more than journalism. He declared that he hated it, and hailed his release from it as a deliverance into life; but he never did anything else so well. In the great days of the *feuilleton* he was a master *feuilletoniste*. His imagination and invention are endless—and, indeed, the serious reader must always make allowances for them. No other of the great musical critics, Schumann or Wagner or Hanslick, had so much humor, so much wit, so much energy and spirit; and none of them showed so much literary brilliancy. His critical insight and capaci-

ties, as well as his knowledge—and some may say
that critical insight, capacities, and knowledge are
the foremost requisites of a great critic—were limited. But he admired and hated magnificently; and
for what he admired and hated he had a unique
power of appraisal and expression. His eloquent
admiration for Gluck, Beethoven, and Weber was
paired with a total inability to perceive Bach, or,
indeed, any other member of the elder schools, as
at all worthy of modern attention. It may be said
that by this very fact he is dated and ranged. Readers of his biography will remember his definition of
a fugue as a composition in which one part chases
another and all together they chase the listener out
of the hall. He wrote a few fugues himself, as in duty
bound, in his "Requiem" and in some other places;
but they are naturally not of his best, and they are
not models for the aspiring contrapuntal student.
And the readers of his biography will also recall
that at another time, when his hosts in a strange
city took him to a concert at which Bach's music
was to be heard, he dryly remarks in his account of
it that he did not suppose they intended to give him
pain. Perhaps Berlioz is the solitary exception to
the statement that Bach has always been the musicians' musician, the one for whom all who have

known his works poured out limitless admiration.
And perhaps this fact in itself is a contribution to
a knowledge and an estimate of Berlioz's musical
nature. Berlioz's writing about the composers whom
he loved is full of good things eloquently stated;
but his view as a critic was singularly limited. Nor
is it necessary to adduce in support of this his curt
and dry dismissal of Wagner. It is needless to expect
impossibilities or to ignore human limitations so far
as to imagine that Berlioz could understand the
greatness of this contemporary—and, after all, in a
certain sense, necessarily a rival—so much greater
than himself, or could admit the possibility of being
overshadowed by a rival at the time hardly more
successful than himself in a worldly way.

His French admirers, especially, bracket him with
Wagner, to make a pair of misunderstood modern
geniuses, scorned by their contemporaries, pro-
scribed in the opera houses of the world, relegated
to a doleful exile, persecuted because they were
working for the future. Such an affecting picture is
always more engaging than the cold facts, which do
not, in all respects, agree with it. Mr. Ernest New-
man has shown that Wagner was by no means pro-
scribed in the opera houses of Germany, from even
his earlier days. Least of all, did he appeal in vain

to the public—not merely to the élite, watching for a new day, but to the great public of his own time and country, who accepted him, though not in all cases by any means at once, with reasonable alacrity and in reasonably large numbers. Berlioz was not accepted at once, undoubtedly, especially in his native land, though he was listened to with interest and admiration across the Rhine. Schumann made himself his champion in the early days; and later he had no more ardent champions than Felix Mottl and Felix Weingartner. Both did much to promote a Berlioz cult in Germany by performing his works; and Weingartner has been one of the editors of the complete edition of Berlioz's works published by the German firm of Breitkopf & Härtel. The writer might add that in a long experience the only opera of Berlioz he ever heard performed was "Benvenuto Cellini," in Dresden, and an operatic setting of "La Damnation de Faust," such as the composer neither expected nor desired, also in New York, in 1906.

But, after all, there was and is no real reason why Berlioz should be accepted eagerly, wholly, and at once. He was not a great composer; and neither then nor since has his music, taken as a whole, fired the imagination or nourished the soul of a world waiting for fire and nourishment. Such acceptance as he has had has been due in great part not to his own qualities as a composer, but to the need in France of a great composer to set over against Wagner; and since Wagner has made his way to unquestioned acceptance in France we hear something less of Berlioz. Let us not forget, says M. Adolphe Boschot, the sufferings, the doubts, and the struggles of the old age of Berlioz, an old age that came too early and lasted too long. We are not likely to, with Berlioz's own vivid exposition of them, or so long as such skilful and eloquent pleaders as M. Boschot appear for him. Yet M. Boschot, it may be thought by readers of his absorbing and delightful biography, "saw through" him in some even of his less transparent poses and attitudes.

Berlioz had some of his earliest recognition in New York. The Philharmonic Society of that city began its career in 1842 with an ardent zeal to make New York familiar not only with the classics but also with the products of the newest impulses of the art of that time. Berlioz came into special favor as a prophet of the new music, perhaps because of the presence in the councils of the Philharmonic of two Frenchmen, Alfred Boucher and D. G. Etienne. In 1846, four years after its foundation, the Philharmonic Society played a piece by Berlioz, the overture to "Les Francs Juges," for the first time in America. Numerous others appeared on its programmes in the next ensuing years; and they were early days in the history of the Berlioz cult. It was a conscientious propaganda that was made for his music. "Le Roi Lear" was played in 1846; "Le Carnaval Romain" in 1861; the "Symphonie Fantastique" in 1866, played again two years later; parts of "Roméo et Juliette" in 1867; selections from "Les Troyens" in 1877. The "Carnaval Romain" and the "Waverley" overtures had been played for the first time in New York in 1856, at Bergmann's concerts; the "Roméo et Juliette" symphony in one of Theodore Thomas's "symphony soirées" in 1867. As conductor of the Brooklyn Philharmonic Society, Thomas gave the "Corsair" overture for the first time in 1863, and the overture to "Benvenuto Cellini," also for the first time, in 1867. Most of these works were several times repeated; and in later years they and others frequently appeared upon New York programmes of the Philharmonic and New York Symphony orchestras. It might be noted, in considering these records in New York, that the name of Berlioz does not appear upon the programmes of the London Philharmonic Society until 1853, the year he was engaged as its conductor; and that it does not appear upon those of the Vienna Philharmonic till 1856, when the great venture was made of playing the "Queen Mab" scherzo. In Paris the records of the Société des Concerts show one performance of "Rob Roy" in 1833 and one of "La Damnation de Faust" in 1849, and then nothing more of Berlioz till 1863.

The overture to "Benvenuto Cellini," the "Carnaval Romain" from the same opera, the three orchestral snippets, "Queen Mab," "Will-o'-the Wisps," and the "Dance of the Sylphs," the orchestral arrangement of the "Rakoczy March," of which only the orchestral garb is Berlioz's, reappear in later days not infrequently on orchestral programmes, especially on those of a "popular" kind. The "Symphonie Fantastique" is occasionally played; the "Harold" symphony even less often. "The Damnation of Faust" is still given, and its best numbers are among the productions of Berlioz, in which the breath of life most inheres; much of it, however, is ready for burial. Occasionally some ambitious conductor makes an attempt to thrill with the "Ninevitish," the "Babylonian" extravagances of the "Te Deum" or the "Requiem"; but modern audiences are much more bored than thrilled by them. We hear something of the beauty and dramatic value of the operas — "The Trojans," "The Trojans in Carthage," "Beatrice and Benedict," "Benvenuti Cellini" — but we do not hear the operas. Operatic managers know better than to attempt them.

Through his critical and polemical writings Berlioz impressed himself and his ideas even more than through his music upon the world of his day. They all show a limitless self-confidence, a boundless ambition to accomplish great and original things in music, a daring that scoffed at precedents and at established conventions. His music is an expression of it all; but it also expresses the impotence of his specifically musical endowment to achieve the vast results he aimed at. He devised thitherto unheard-of ways and means to embody those results. We are given grandiose and all-embracing schemes; projects of mythological, "Asiatic" magnificence. We are told of the imaginative, poetical, tender, tragical, ironical, horrible chapters that are to live in his music. We listen to effect piled upon effect; we admire the technical skill, at least in the writing for the orchestra; but we are left cold. The mountain labors, but rarely does it bring forth more than a musical mouse.

Berlioz To-day

Berlioz's musical thought is almost always superficial. His musical invention is terribly, wearisomely commonplace. How few of the themes in any of his most important compositions are expressive or beautiful, or find their way to the heart! The pomp and glitter and the wealth of color with which he sets them forth can only hide their poverty. How pale and poor is the "idée fixe" of the "Fantastic Symphony"; how inexpressive the cantilena of the "Benvenuto Cellini" overture! Think of the thematic wanderings of the "Harold Symphony," the empty pomposities of much of the "Te Deum" and the "Requiem Mass." They are, typical of the composer's lack of invention of a purely musical sort. They cannot be offset by memories of the love music of the "Roméo et Juliette" symphony; or the several appealing numbers of "La Damnation de Faust"; or the pallid charm of the "Scene in the Fields," or the pretty ball-room music, both in the "Fantastic Symphony"; or the vivacity and life of "The Roman Carnival" overture.

Yet so penetrating a critic as Sir W. H. Hadow, writing thirty and more years ago, considers that Berlioz has left us "some tunes of very high worth." He considers "La Captive" to be "a complete and final answer to the critics who have regarded the composer as unmelodious"; he calls the love scene in "Roméo et Juliette" as beautiful as an adagio of Schubert; and he mentions further the septet in "Les Troyens," the shepherds' chorus in "The Childhood of Christ," Hero's Song, "Je Vais le Voir," in "Béatrice et Bénédict," the Sanctus in the "Requiem" as "sufficient to place him incontrovertibly in the first rank of musicians." Are they more than lucky exceptions? It is true that composers, like other artists, ought to be judged by the best they have done rather than by their worst, or perhaps even their average. It is a pity that these outstanding inspirations have not, for the most part, had vitality enough to maintain themselves alive in modern programmes. It may be that, as Francis Hueffer, another English critic, has put it, "the equation between matter and manner in his work is a question of chance, not of choice."

Berlioz's deficiency as a harmonist not less than as a melodist is one that sensibly estranges the modern listener from his work. His harmony rarely rises above the commonplace, the insipid. It is colorless. He had little feeling for the expressive emotional power that is so eloquent in chromatic harmony and in the modern use of discord, both of which are

among the most characteristic tokens of the music
following Berlioz for fifty years. His harmony seems
often to have no organic connection with his melody, to be no necessary and inevitable ground-
work for it. His treatment is obvious until he makes
some sudden and remote modulation that carries
him far afield, yet without direct significance or apparent inner necessity. He "changes his key with
a forcible wrench that surprises without pleasing";
he is "so suspicious of monotony that he falls into
restlessness." If Saint-Saëns's dictum is true, that
the men who find beautiful melodies are the ones also
who find beautiful harmonies, the application of
its converse to Berlioz is evident. His mastery of
rhythm may be granted and gives point to many
things that have little other significance. As for his
ideas of form, they are often, as it seems, purposely
vague, and lead him to rambling repetitions and to
uncertainty of outline in many of his larger works,
especially the so-called symphonic movements. We
are no longer affrighted by freedom of form, provided it is the embodiment of an inward necessity;
nor at elaborate and complicated means of expression, if they only succeed in expressing; nor at
vast designs, ambitions, the heaven-storming attempts, such as Berlioz's, to put into music all the

extremes of human emotion, passion, and experience, if we only really find them there. To these things we are inured. What we are not inured to is the failure of so many of Berlioz's attempts, the baroque triviality, the little significance in much sound.

Berlioz's credit as the originator of the modern orchestra and of some of the most significant developments of programme music is still maintained. His instrumentation may sound in places—and the places are increasing to the modern ear in number and extent—a little hard, glittering, hollow, "wire-edged," without real warmth or depth of color. There is still much of it that the most accomplished modern skill cannot surpass in sheer brilliancy, in subtle refinement, in the expressive use of instrumental timbres for special effects. And the full value of it all cannot be grasped without remembering that it was as a pioneer that Berlioz worked in this field. But there are those who doubt the extent of Berlioz's influence as an orchestral innovator on his contemporaries and successors. They deny that Wagner learned his orchestral technique or any considerable part of it, from Berlioz, and point out essential differences in the methods of the two men and the resulting effects of their orchestration. They point to Berlioz's "Treatise on Orchestration" as something from which not much that is tangible or applicable to modern orchestral technique is to be learned. You will find there, they say, sympathetic and interesting remarks about the tonal colors and qualities of the several instruments in extraordinary and exceptional uses; curious researches into some of the bizarre effects that his predecessors and he himself attempted. Thus he mentions M. Langlois's ingenious procedure on the double-bass, in producing sounds that would admirably supply the orchestra with the representation of "a loud female cry." He expatiates upon the advantage of the melancholy and dreamy character of the guitar— "which might more frequently be made available" —to which instrument he devotes many pages: it was the only one on which he himself was a performer. He more than once emphasized the fact that only those who play it can write really well for it, also mentions the "singular property" of the guitar, which, unlike the majority of instruments, loses by being employed in numbers; for the sound of twelve guitars playing in unison is "almost absurd." He explains the mistake that some great writers, Mozart among them, have made in urging the oboe to utterance of "passion, anger, menace, or heroism." He esteems the kettle-drums highly, and cannot refrain from enlarging on the admirable effect in his " Requiem " of eight pairs of them tuned differently, and played with different results with different kinds of drum-sticks. He celebrates the beauties of bells; the voluptuous delicacy of the keyed harmonica, the wonderful possibilities of the cymbals, especially of the small cymbals of antiquity; the extraordinary effect of the "long drum" in his "Requiem" giving the idea of "the strange and awful noises that accompany great cataclysms of nature," magnificent and powerful effect of eight, ten, twelve, or more drums. And then there is the delectable invention, of which we to-day are only too well aware, of Mr. Adolphe Sax: the six kinds of saxophones, — Mr. Sax being then about to bless the world with a seventh. What a marvel of prophecy and far-seeing vision this is: "Clever composers will hereafter derive wondrous effects from saxophones associated with the clarinet family, or introduced in other combinations!" He sets forth his plan of a monster orchestra to include all the players in Paris, of which he gives overwhelming details; beginning with 120 violins and including 12 bassoons, 16 horns, 30 harps, 30 pianofortes, 8 pairs of kettle-drums played by 10 drummers, 6 triangles, 1 organ, 6 sets of bells, 12 pairs of ancient cymbals, and so on: 467 instrumentalists. The proportions seem in some instances eccentric; are they determined by the number of players upon certain instruments that happened to be then in Paris? Fortunately, though composers have in the last hundred years or so increased their demands for orchestral sonorities, the art of orchestral writing has not developed toward anything like this; and Berlioz's instrumental ecstasies are still admired only at a distance. The more pedestrian composers, whose chief idea is not to affright or subdue the world, still find it advisable to look elsewhere.

Perhaps many who came after him who have played a prominent part in modern art, are to some extent in debt to the ideals that Berlioz set up and tried, himself, so hard to realize. But that cannot blind us to the sight of his ambition panting in vain behind his intentions, and never able to catch up. His influence has been rather through the potency of his intellectual processes than by his musical embodiment of them.

CAMILLE SAINT–SAËNS

WITH the death of Camille Saint-Saëns, on December 16, 1921, disappeared one of the few remaining links connecting the present with a past in music that some insist upon thinking is the more glorious. Saint-Saëns himself was very certain of it. He set his face resolutely against most of the latest developments of musical art. He said comparatively little about them, but his scorn and dislike of them are sufficiently recorded: generally in more or less allusive and left-handed passages; in a few cases more incisively and at length. For Saint-Saëns was not only a fertile and unwearied composer, producing new works almost up to the year of his death; he was also most articulate in a literary way—a clear thinker, a pungent writer, a sharp critic, who had traversed not only his own art of music minutely but was also not averse to thinking of other things as well, whereby he was distinguished from many of his profession. His published works are an attestation of his vigor as a thinker and of his power as a writer.

When he first came to America, in the autumn of 1906, a notable event in American musical annals, he was properly greeted at a concert of the New York Symphony Orchestra in Carnegie Hall by a very large audience, with a spontaneous and enthusiastic welcome, and with a fanfare by the orchestra. He came upon the platform an elderly gentleman of 71 years, short of stature but robust in figure, of quick and rather precise movements, gray-bearded but darkly thatched, except for an oncoming bald spot; whose face, with its striking aquiline nose, had long been familiar from his portraits. Acquaintance with his music in New York had preceded his coming by many years; it was not increased in any important degree by the performance in which he took part as a pianist. He presented himself as a pianoforte virtuoso and played three pieces, adding then another, which, all practically unknown in New York, had small claim to be set forth as really representative of his quality as a composer. He had the name of an adept at orchestral conducting; but he was not called upon to conduct his symphonic poem, "Le Rouet d'Omphale," which the orchestra played. At his second concert he played his pianoforte concerto in G minor, and took the organ part in his symphony in C minor, and in his early serenade Op. 15. At the third he played his fifth pianoforte concerto in F, Op. 103, then heard probably for the first time in New York; a piece composed by him for the fiftieth anniversary of his first appearance as a public pianist, which was celebrated in Paris in 1896. Then he gave a pianoforte recital, with what was noted at the time as a "quaint" programme, such as no modern pianist would dream of putting forward. Finally, he conducted an orchestral concert, rather an unfortunate affair, in which his conducting was "smooth, even, and graceful, seldom dynamic. He held his baton rather stiffly and contented himself with pointing out nuances and effects with the least possible effort." As a pianist his playing was found to be full of charm and of remarkable facility, when his years were considered —and it was necessary to consider them. There were sparkling clearness, elegance, and grace in his rippling passages and runs. He phrased and sang a melody with distinction and point; and all was done with perfect repose, though on a somewhat miniature scale and within restricted limits of dynamic contrast and tonal color. Little that he played called for eloquence or for feeling that even scratched the surface; and he gave no sign of either. His most important performance was of his G minor concerto. It would have been unfair to compare this performance with that of a young man in the plenitude of his strength—and few are the younger virtuosos who had not at some time played it in

Camille Saint-Saëns

New York. Dr. Saint-Saëns at 71 had no longer the power to produce upon the piano a tone to cope with that of the orchestra. But under the circumstances it was a remarkable performance; it was remarkable for the clearness and cogency with which he expounded the themes of the first movement, even though he did not reveal fully the breadth and power of the opening improvisation in the manner of Bach; remarkable also in the clearness and vivacity and sparkle of the brilliant passage work of the last two movements. He seemed at times to be carried away by the impetuosity of the music; the phrasing was now and then slighted, to the detriment of the rhythm; yet the grace of those themes, captivating in their way, has not often been more persuasively presented. In his recital he played Bach and Rameau with delightful repose, clearness, and polish of style. In his Chopin (the "Barcarolle") there were finish and transparency; but it was a sober Chopin, in a very cool, dry light.

In 1915 he came again to America—now eighty years old—as a member of a French committee to represent France at the Panama-Pacific Exposition in San Francisco. One of his contributions to that occasion was a "Hymn to California," which he composed for the Exposition. His days as a performer were, of course, over; but he received the honor due him for his eminence and as a representative of France at a critical time. It cannot be said that the "Hymn to California" was an important addition to the tale of his works or that it made even a passing ripple upon the surface of musical art. He was then little more than a picturesque figure with an aureole; an artist *emeritus*.

Saint-Saëns's music had long been known in New York before he set foot on the American shore; and his position as a great force in the musical activities of his native land was recognized. There was no department of music to which he had not made numerous and important contributions, except that of the string quartet. The restless activity that brought him to America in his seventy-second year, and again in his eightieth, was a manifestation of the same ceaseless stirring of soul that kept him unwearied in the composition of music till almost the year of his death, in 1922, at the age of eighty-seven. Musicians are playing with almost undiminished zest numerous compositions of his that have been in the repertory half a century and more. It is a long span; and it was a rich and varied career unfolded in the more than seventy-four years that elapsed between his first publications as a composer and his death.

Camille Saint-Saëns

Saint-Saëns was truly a representative of the Gallic spirit, not only in his music but also in his personality, his many-sided culture, the brilliancy and grace and effectiveness with which his intellect was brought to play upon whatever interested it; also, it may be said, in a certain sort of logical dryness, of academic formality that marked him. As a writer of criticism, keen and of wide sympathies in certain directions, he had emphatic aversions. He delighted in paradox; and more than once, having espoused the cause of the under dog, he turned and rent that same, when he became the upper dog; as when, in the earlier days, he wrote urgently in favor of the later dramas of Wagner, only to discover, after Wagner had won the day in France, that his music was no food for French taste. He dabbled in astronomy, in mathematics, in psychology. He interested himself in archaeology; and was zealous in reviving—so far as modern performances may be called revival —the classical drama, with music, in the old Roman theatres of France, as in those of Béziers, Nîmes, and Arles. He travelled in many lands; and stories of his disappearances, sometimes at critical moments, have been amusingly exaggerated. One of these stories even has it that years ago Saint-Saëns came *incognito* to New York and spent some days at a

French hotel there, where he was recognized by a compatriot. But there has never been any sufficient corroboration of this.

Saint-Saëns, like most other musicians who have risen to lasting distinction, was a "wonder-child." He began to learn the piano at the age of two and a half years. Some of his later autobiographical chapters give amusing records of his childhood musicianship. He made his first appearance publicly as a pianist in his eleventh year. He studied at the Conservatoire in Paris and won a prize in organ playing, but failed to gain the Roman prize. His first fame, that endured through all that came to him since, was that of a virtuoso on the pianoforte and organ. He was especially noted as a sight reader of the most difficult and complicated scores, and from the most undecipherable manuscripts; and those who have witnessed what he could do in this way have been able to compare him only with Liszt. There is a story of his calling at Wahnfried and while waiting for "the Master" to descend, dashing off on the pianoforte a scene from "Siegfried," still unpublished and in the composer's manuscript; and another of his calling on Tausig, who was working on his pianoforte arrrangement of "Die Meister-singer," and who heard the visitor waiting for him in his music room reading over the orchestral score on the pianoforte; and rushing in with his collar still unbuttoned to see who could accomplish such wonders, found Saint-Saëns.

Saint-Saëns's music has formed an indispensable part of the modern repertory in almost all the branches of the art. His "Samson et Dalila" has been an important item in the operatic seasons, here and elsewhere; his C minor symphony has been regularly on the programmes of the orchestras— perhaps not so much lately as in former years; the symphony in A is still played in New York; his violin concerto, his "Rondo Capriccioso," and his "Havanaise" are valuable to the violin virtuoso, as his pianoforte concertos in G minor and C minor— the former a little less now than formerly—are to the pianist, and his 'cello concerto to the 'cellist. It is not long since his symphonic poems "Le Rouet d'Omphale," "Danse Macabre," "La Jeunesse d'Hercule," and "Phaëthon," and his "Suite Algérienne" were valued on orchestral programmes more than they are at present. Violinists still play the arrangement of the prelude to "Le Déluge" and 'cellists the piece entitled "Le Cygne" (originally a serious number in his jocose fantasy, "Le Carnaval des Animaux"). A number of his brilliant pianoforte pieces are not forgotten. His songs, with a few exceptions, have never been much sung here; nor have his operas, except "Samson et Dalila," ever had a long life upon the stage, as have the works of many men in certain respects his inferiors who have had more of dramatic blood. "Samson et Dalila" had rather a curious history in its inception. Saint-Saëns began it in 1869, when he was chiefly known as an instrumental composer and was likewise, after the French custom of the time, considered very "Wagnerian" in his tendencies. Under these circumstances he could have very little hope of seeing his work accepted at the Opéra. (As a matter of fact, its first operatic performance was in Weimar in 1877 and it did not reach the Opéra in Paris till 1892.) Anticipating such a fate for "Samson et Dalila," Saint-Saëns deliberately and with all forethought constructed the work so that it would do as well on the concert stage as an oratorio as on the operatic stage as an opera; and its first performances in New York were as an oratorio. There is needed no great acumen to see that it is better suited to the concert stage than to the operatic.

Not one of his dozen operas has the spark of life except "Samson et Dalila." They have been spasmodically revived in Paris since their composer attained to his unquestioned preëminence among the living; but none of them could ever last out more than a few performances, with a success hardly of "esteem." Most people have to endure a good deal to get through with "Samson," especially its first and third acts, getting little from it except the famous contralto air in the third act and the somewhat less famous one in the first. The music chills by its scholastic sobriety, the drama by its lack of forward movement. There is a great deal for the chorus—as befits a work meant for alternative use as an oratorio—largely in the contrapuntal style and in part such as might come out of the synagogue. The libretto—it was written by a cousin of Saint-Saëns—is hardly more dramatic than those of his other operas. For one of his intelligence, Saint-Saëns was satisfied with incredibly poor librettos.

It was Saint-Saëns's fortune to do more than any other since Berlioz to cultivate and foster the composition of instrumental music in France, where music so long stood in the general estimation for opera and for very little else, and where the sole ambition of most musicians was to succeed in opera. "You are less unfortunate than I," Bizet used to tell him, as Saint-Saëns relates in his book, "L'Ecole Buissonière"; "you can do something besides things

for the stage; I can't. That is my only resource."
There were not many others who could, in Saint-
Saëns's adolescent days; but that state of things is
past, and it was in large part owing to Saint-Saëns
and his work that it is past.

The span of his musical composition covers a
period of seventy years, his Opus 1 ("Trois Mor-
ceaux pour Harmonium") having been composed in
1852 and published in 1858; his first symphony,
composed in 1853, was published in 1855. His second concerto, in G minor, was composed and published in 1868, his "Rondo Capriccioso" was composed in 1863. It is a remarkable record; a record
that attests the vitality of certain of his compositions in a manner that cannot be gainsaid. There
is not much music of the sixties of the last century
that is still played, except the works of composers
generally recognized as of the very first rank. Of his
very large output, what has survived is not to be de-
spised in quantity. It is, perhaps, as large in proportion to the whole as that which has survived from
the output of many much greater men among the
moderns, with the exception of Brahms and Wagner. Think of the neglected work—a good deal of it
justly neglected—surviving only in the thematic
catalogues, of Mozart, Haydn, Beethoven, Schubert,

Camille Saint-Saëns

Weber, Schumann! To be carried on in the memories of living men by more or less frequent performances of eight or ten capital works is, in truth, almost to taste immortality.

And yet most will hesitate to put Saint-Saëns seriously very near the first rank. His music has invention, skill, ingenuity, taste, a great feeling for form and for rhythm, mastery of resource for all the mediums in which he wrote—practically every medium except that of the string quartet; though he did compose an unimportant work in that form. But there is rarely in it a true creative force, passion, warmth, and vivifying power, or even spontaneity. There is always the impression of accomplished craftsmanship, of expertness, as the underlying source of it all — and they are not enough. He was an "eclectic" rather than a potent originality. He lacked the flame of a vivifying imagination.

It was not long before his death that Saint-Saëns wrote, denying the thesis that music is "all expression and passion," saying: "To me art is form above all else. . . . The artist who does not feel thoroughly satisfied with elegant lines, harmonious colors, or a fine series of chords does not understand art. When beautiful forms accompany powerful expression we are filled with admiration, and rightly so. In such a case, what is it that happens? Our cravings for art and emotion are alike satisfied. All the same, we cannot, therefore, say that we have reached the summit of art, for art is capable of existing apart from the slightest trace of emotion or passion. . . . Music is not the 'vapeur d'art'; it is a plastic art—one that is made up of forms."

In these words Saint-Saëns has explained himself and his music perfectly. He himself seldom rose to the height of great emotion or powerful expression. You will find it, perhaps—or is it only a semblance? —in the song of Dalila, "Mon Cœur s'ouvre à ta Voix," but you will also find that the opera, or oratorio, is almost written around this one fortunate idea, to give it a frame and setting. And you will find it with similar or greater rarity in other of his works. His piercing intelligence, his all-embracing understanding of his art are never found lacking in his music. It is always made with a great skill in the adaptation of means to the end, with an unerring touch and treatment. He has the right expression for everything; there are no exaggeration, no forced contrasts, no rioting amid the new orchestral colors and the lush harmonies of modern times. Yet he had a fine sense of tonal color and a keen instinct for instrumental expression. As Dr. Neitzel, one of his biographers (a German critic), has said: "There are few places where the ear is not delighted by the manner in which his music is put upon the instruments, whether in a register of special tonal charm or through certain color combinations, or through dynamic nuances and their thousandfold relations." It is a much-abused word; but for whatever instrument Saint-Saëns wrote, he wrote "idiomatically"; his musical thoughts are conceived in terms of the medium through which they are to be expressed, whether it is the voice, the pianoforte, the strings, the wind instruments, the orchestra, or the chorus. He had, too, a charming, clear-cut sense of rhythm; and a rich inventiveness in this direction. The allegiance that Saint-Saëns yielded to Bach has often been commented on; and there are many passages that suggest a sort of assimilation of Bach's modes of expression. All will remember the grandiose opening of the G minor pianoforte concerto; and there are movements in several of the chamber compositions, as well as in some of the choral works that will impress the hearer as an echo of Bach's style. And the source of Saint-Saëns's skilful and plastic counterpoint, even when this counterpoint is not so plainly marked with the formal characteristics of Bach's art, is not to be mistaken.

Musical Discourse

Clear and transparent his writing always is, and marked by restraint in all things; by balance and proportion in form, by fertile ingenuity in workmanship. But it is in the specific musical invention, without which all these things are as sounding brass and tinkling cymbals; in melodic utterance that warms and touches the heart; in passion and eloquence and in the highest attributes of sheer beauty, that Saint-Saëns's music is so often lacking. "Art is capable of existing apart from the slightest trace of emotion or passion"—an "oratio pro domo sua"! It is often said that his music is dry. It is the dryness of abstraction, of preoccupation with method, of the lack of much that is really vital in matter. How rarely did he hit upon what seemed formerly a sumptuous and convincing passage, such as the now hackneyed air of Dalila in "Samson et Dalila"! How many of his themes are cold and gray, lacking emotional appeal; and how often is the intelligence of the listener beguiled with a movement of impeccable skill and ingenuity to which the heart has refused to yield conviction! But this is only to say, after all, that the artist lacks the true creative power and has substituted therefor the dry husks of training and dexterity; that the ultimate gift of genius has been denied him. Yet Saint-Saëns, even at the

Camille Saint-Saëns

time of his death, was one of the impressive figures
in the world of music, for the qualities he possessed,
for the work he had done; a most characteristic figure, indeed, of French art in a period now closed.

JENNY LIND AND BARNUM

THE history of one of the grandest achievements of the press agent—all the grander considering the early and comparatively primitive days in which it occurred—was recalled in New York in 1920, when Mme. Frieda Hempel appeared in her "Jenny Lind concert" in Carnegie Hall. It commemorated the hundredth anniversary of the great Swedish singer's birth, reviving at the same time memories of her first appearance in the United States seventy years before. It was a reproduction, so far as the records, aided by a more or less creative imagination, could enable it to be effected, of Jenny Lind's first concert in New York at Castle Garden, on September 11, 1850. The programme of that concert was repeated with the exception of one number, the music of which appeared to be at the present time unobtainable. The artists who took part in the concert presented themselves in the costumes of the period, headed by Mme. Hempel, one of the few sopranos extant who could rightfully claim to represent Jenny Lind's art. She was a golden-haired vision, very like a Swedish nightingale in white satin crinoline, garlanded with morning-glories. There were representatives of Signor Beletti, the baritone of Jenny Lind's company; of Julius Benedict, her conductor, and of Richard

Hoffman, her pianist. There was an orchestra; and all wore the costumes of 1850, some looking uncomfortable. Over the platform was an illuminated inscription, as there was in Castle Garden seventy years before, "Welcome, Sweet Warbler." P. T. Barnum, Jenny Lind's manager, made his appearance in a more or less plausible impersonation. Several firemen, in fire hats and red shirts and with brass trumpets, moved about the hall, remnant of the force of 700 that Barnum's genius evoked to escort the Swedish singer from the steamer on her arrival. A couple of old square pianos stood on the stage for the two-piano duet that was played, and a still older piano was provided for Mme. Hempel to play her own accompaniment on in the "Swedish Herdsman's Song" that was included in the programme.

It is interesting to recall the programme: the overture to Weber's "Oberon"; the scena and cavatina "Casta Diva" from Bellini's "Norma"; the air "Largo al Factotum" from Rossini's "Barber of Seville"; the "Herdsman's Song" that concert singers still affect, "Kom Kyria," were all music that had survived the seventy years. Perhaps some had heard the trio for soprano and two flutes, "composed expressly for Jenny Lind," by Meyerbeer, in his opera of "The Camp in Silesia" (afterwards recast as "L'Etoile du Nord"). But who could have identified the baritone air "Sorgete," from Rossini's opera of "Maometto Secondo," the duet for soprano and baritone, "Pei Piacere alla Signora" from his opera of "Il Turco in Italia," the overture to "The Crusaders" by Julius Benedict, or the setting by the same composer of the prize poem by Bayard Taylor, "The Greeting to America," composed at Barnum's instigation for this occasion? The programme went astray in its mention of the duet for two pianos, which was not by Benedict, as stated, but was originally Thalberg's Fantasia on airs from Bellini's "Norma." That classic had somehow failed to survive in any obtainable form, however; and the two pianists had perforce to play a more modern piece, doubtless to the greater edification of the audience. Some might inquire whether, as a matter of history, this duet was played at Castle Garden on two square pianos, in view of the fact that in 1850 the grand piano was a well-established institution and the American pioneer piano-makers had already introduced their share of the improvements that made possible the instruments of to-day.

The concert of which this was a recognizable reproduction not only introduced a great singer to America, but also registered a high-water mark in

Jenny Lind and Barnum

P. T. Barnum's fame which he scarcely surpassed in all his subsequent years of triumph. Reverberations of the original achievement rolling down the corridors of fifty years served to advance the fortunes of the "Jenny Lind Charities"—the institutions which Jenny Lind, on the advice of the Mayor of New York, selected in 1850 as the beneficiaries of her first American concert. Whatever they may be at present, they were then numerous and were copiously nurtured half a century ago by the kindly hand of the Swedish singer, one of the most charitable of artists.

Indeed, though it may sound shabby to mention it now, this charitable disposition, with due and extensive advertising of it, was one of the elements of Jenny Lind's nature that P.T. Barnum counted most upon to arouse the sympathy and admiration of the American public, and thus to increase the size and profitableness of the audiences at her concerts. He tells in his autobiography, with perfect frankness and without a touch of conscious cynicism, how he capitalized this benevolent spirit in his calculations for his enterprise:

"I relied largely on Jenny Lind's reputation as a great artist; also took largely into my estimate of her success her character for extraordinary benevolence and generosity. Without this peculiarity of her disposition I should never have dared to make the engagement."

And so charity concerts were carefully provided for in the contract. He relates how, seeing the great success that was sure to attend the first concert, after all the well-known advertising schemes were going on so well, and the distinguished hatter had bought the first ticket for $225, he announced that her share of the first two concerts would be devoted to charity and the sum was put at $50,000. But as her own share was too small to make this up, they agreed to waive the terms of the contract for these two concerts, divide the proceeds equally, and not to reckon them in the number provided for in the agreement.

Jenny Lind was fairness itself in regard to the charity department of the business. She remonstrated with Barnum, he says, at the terms applicable to subsequent charity concerts, saying that the expenses should be deducted from her share and that, as things were, he was giving more than she was from the proceeds of them, while she got the credit. But Barnum, though he was not in business as a philanthropist, saw money rolling his way in such streams as no American "amusement enterprise," probably, had ever before gathered; and saw, also, that it was well to go on as he had begun. So he benevolently declined to make any change. The table he gives in his book of the charity donations forms an impressive tribute to the astuteness of his original premises, taken in connection with the table of receipts for the concerts.

But when it came to the purely business end of the contract, when there was no charity to be considered and when the accounts were not to be exploited for advertising purposes, Jenny Lind saw things in a little different light. Some of the reports have it that when she perceived how much money there was going to be in the affair, she went to Barnum and flatly repudiated her contract, telling him coolly that she must have a more favorable one. He, in his autobiography, gives himself the credit of proposing the revision. He says that when he did so, she grasped his hand and said, "Mr. Barnum, you are a gentleman of honor. You are generous. I will sing for you anywhere." This at least makes a story more creditable to both. Other and perhaps more accurate accounts say that when Jenny Lind became dissatisfied with her contract, when she saw how the money was pouring into her manager's purse, she wanted a revision of it, not only once but "again and again"; and Barnum, apparently all complaisance and liberality, yielded. It was, of course, the part of wisdom for him to keep her contented, for a dissatisfied prima donna, wanting her freedom, would not have been a great asset for a manager. Barnum, inveterately modest, goes on to say that his alleged offer of an increase was not wholly an act of generosity, for he had become convinced that "there was money enough in the enterprise for all of us"; and thought that while Jenny ought to be satisfied with the original terms, "envious persons" would try to make her discontented, and that it would be a stroke of policy to prevent the possibility of such an occurrence.

But, surely enough, envious persons got to work on her later. By the next May her "advisers," as Barnum calls them, had persuaded her to cut loose from him. At her eighty-fifth concert she told him that she had decided to pay the $25,000 forfeit provided for in the contract for its cancellation, and to close the tour with the hundredth concert, instead of the hundred and fiftieth. At the ninety-third concert Barnum offered to relinquish his interest if she would pay him $1,000 apiece for managing the remaining seven, besides the forfeit. This she accepted. Thereafter she gave concerts on her

own responsibility, as Barnum somewhat sardoni-
cally reports, "with varying success." She com-
plained to him that she had been sadly harassed by
people cheating her. But she always sent Barnum
complimentary tickets to her concerts whenever he
was about.

Barnum published a table of his receipts, not
under oath nor certified by chartered public ac-
countants, but doubtless near enough to the truth.
By this it appears that the highest records for single
concerts were made in New Orleans, $12,599; Rich-
mond, $12,385; and Cincinnati, $11,001. In New
York his total receipts, after the deductions provided for, were for 100 concerts, $176,675. Barnum's
total gross receipts for ninety-five concerts were
$712,161; he does not give his net profits. Jenny
Lind's net proceeds were $176,675, after she had
paid her forfeit of $25,000. The distinguished hatter
of New York who paid $225 for the first ticket in
Castle Garden was quite eclipsed when the tour
began. In Providence an eager gentleman paid $653;
and in Boston others of the same stripe paid $625
each.

To lay the foundations of his advertising, Barnum
got Jenny Lind to give two concerts in Liverpool
on the eve of her departure for America. He had

"procured the services of a musical critic from London," as he says, who "finished his account of this concert at half past one o'clock the same night"— rapid, industrious, and no doubt judicially impartial critic!—and at two o'clock Barnum's agent was overseeing its insertion in a Liverpool morning paper, numbers of which he forwarded to the manager in America, by the steamer of the same day. Musical critics and morning newspapers seem to have been singularly obliging in those times; and it is gratifying to learn that the republication of this critical article in the American press had "the desired effect."

On her arrival in New York, Jenny Lind found triumphal arches on the wharf, inscribed " Welcome Jenny Lind" and "Welcome to America." As Barnum genially remarks in his book, these were probably not produced by magic. Jenny Lind was innocently puzzled to understand, on her travels, how the crowds always knew the time of her arrival in the different towns she visited. Barnum confesses to less astonishment. But the crowds always responded. In Philadelphia, as he relates, the crowd demanded her appearance on the balcony of her hotel. She had a headache; and to avoid disturbing her Barnum got her companion, Miss Ahmansen, to put on the singer's bonnet and shawl and led her to the balcony, where she bowed gracefully, and the crowd dispersed after giving three cheers. He "never dared tell Jenny," he says; but he neglects to say that this trick was found out, and reports of it got about so that in other cities crowds demanding Jenny Lind refused to be satisfied with her bonnet and shawl on another woman.

In New York, according to *The Tribune*, which printed a couple of columns about her every day for weeks, when "space" meant more than it does to-day, crowds wanted to pay their respects to Jenny Lind at the Irving House; but she refused to receive them. Instead, she made an excursion to Greenwood Cemetery. Presents were showered upon her — books, hats, shoes, bouquets, riding equipment. Genin, the distinguished hatter, sent her a riding hat, gloves, and whip; and she is frequently reported as enjoying rides — which, it may be explained for the present generation, meant rides on horseback.

The Tribune's critic went to the rehearsal before the first concert and somewhat indiscreetly, it would be thought now, burst into print about it:

"We went there by no means prejudiced in her favor. We have returned another man. We were cool and unprejudiced; but she completely disarmed us of criticism. . . . In the *trio concertante* with two flutes and voice the orchestra came to a dead stop. They had been listening to the vocalist and forgot their parts."

In this trio, we are told, her voice not only could not be distinguished from the flute, but was absolutely an improvement upon it! This criticism after the concert fills two columns.

The Boston newspapers were in the meantime viewing critically and with disapproval all this pother in New York, as they had, and perhaps even now have, a habit of doing. But when Jenny Lind reached Boston *The Tribune* had opportunity for a little sarcasm:

"Alas for Boston! After all their grave rebukes, their earnest Puritan remonstrances against the honors paid to Mlle. Lind in this city, they have shown very strikingly their superior dignity and severity of demeanor since the arrival of the Nightingale among them. There is but one theme in the Boston papers. Of a verity, the Boston folks are mad. Truly we can understand and sympathize with the strange witchcraft to which our brethren have fallen victims; so did not they with ourselves in the beginning. . . . We told you so!"

Jenny Lind and Barnum

A well-known anecdote relates how Daniel Webster came to New York and heard her at one of her Tripler Hall concerts, having previously called upon her and deeply impressed her in Boston. When his expressed wish to hear "one of the simple mountain airs of her native land" was reported to her in the green room, Jenny Lind obliged with one; whereupon Webster rose in his seat and bowed to her in his largest and most magisterial manner. Another distinguished American statesman heard her in Washington — an aged man feebly advancing to his seat in front, as the audience shouted and applauded; and Julius Benedict bowed, thinking it was all for his performance of the overture. But it was not for him; and as the aged man sank down into his chair, the audience watched him in silence, till one in the gallery shouted, "Three cheers for Harry Clay." The next day Clay called upon her, as did many other statesmen in the capital.

As is well known, Miss Lind married her accompanist, Otto Goldschmidt (who had displaced Julius Benedict), in Boston on February 5, 1852. It had been observed before that date that she "pushed young Goldschmidt"; she put him for two performances on each programme. According to some newspaper accounts the audience thought it a bore and was disposed to guy him by excessive applause of an ironical kind. But can any musical artist think any applause of himself excessive, or hear any "irony" in it? It was not excessive for him, or for Jenny Lind, who listened at the door and "led him off with an air quite beautiful to behold."

The Hoffman who played a pianoforte duet with Julius Benedict at her first concert in Castle Garden and became a member of her traveling company was Richard Hoffman, afterwards one of the best known and best beloved of New York musicians. He writes interestingly of this episode in his book called "Musical Recollections"; in which he says that, of course, no other performance than the singing of Mlle. Lind counted for anything in the concerts, and that the "Fantasia" by Thalberg or themes from "Norma," which he played with Benedict, was hardly listened to. But it gave Hoffman a start in his career, which, he says — and not every public performer would acknowledge so much — many years of ordinary concert playing never could have done. He remembered Jenny Lind's voice as "not so brilliant as deliciously rounded and of exquisite musical timbre," possessing great volume and what seemed an inexhaustible reserve force. "Nothing could have been more naïve and charming than her manner on the stage. She would trip on and off as if in an ecstasy of delight at the opportunity of singing, bowing and smiling to her audience and giving every one present a flattering sense of contributing in a measure toward the success of the evening."

There were a few, a very few, dissenting voices in America. Mr. Werner, in his life of Barnum, quotes Walt Whitman—whose authority in music may not be considered unimpeachable—as saying that Jenny Lind never appealed to his heart in the least. He wondered at her dexterity and her "vocal leaps and double somersets"; but "it was a failure, for there was a vacuum in the head of the performance." The elderly Washington Irving confessed to being one of her admirers; but could not say "how much of his admiration went to her singing, how much to herself."

Apparently Jenny Lind wore out her American welcome after a year or so. It could hardly be expected to keep up to the temperature and tension it had at first. This was partly owing to the lack of Barnum's master hand in guidance; but more to the fact that the novelty had gone and also, perhaps, that personal perfection had begun to pall and there was some weariness at hearing Aristides called the just. Also, Otto Goldschmidt was found a tiresome

element in the programmes. Some of her most ardent
newspaper partisans turned against her. She gave
sometimes unmistakable indications of vexation
when audiences were not so large as they had been.
A Philadelphia newspaper, in December, 1851, remarked that few would regret her determination to
give no more concerts in Philadelphia "unless she
should be able to better suppress the evidences of
ill temper and vexation. She looked as stingey [*i.e.*,
not miserly, but disposed to sting] as a hive of wasps
and as black as a thunder cloud, and all because the
house was not crowded." *The New York Herald*, on
the morning of her departure for Europe, said:
"She has been principally engaged in singing pieces
of opera and catches of all kinds [what kind of
"catches" could they have been?] which were considerably more of the claptrap style than in accordance with the rigid rules of classical music. When
she returns to London and makes her reappearance
in opera [which, of course, she did not do nor intend
to do] she will have to prune away a great deal of
her *ad libitum* redundancies in which she has indulged during her career in this land." This, as Mr.
Werner points out, was the same *Herald* that a year
before had found her song "melting into the song
of the seraphim" until it was "lost in eternity."

Jenny Lind and Barnum

Of course all this excitement over Jenny Lind in America was nothing new; the way had been well prepared in Europe. Benjamin Lumley, the manager who brought Jenny Lind to England and, with less exertion and less of the showman's resource, perhaps, but with no less astuteness than Barnum's, secured her wonderful success there, candidly observes in his autobiography, too, that her grand professional success was aided, no doubt, by the prestige thrown around "the fair Swede," by the "interesting details given to the public of her private life." "The report of her unblemished character, of her unbounded charities, and of her modesty—a modesty that seemed to guard her against the indulgence of personal vanity—added greatly to the favor with which she was received by the English public and gave increased lustre to her professional reputation."

Her success in England had been quite as great as that which she afterwards achieved in America. The newspapers of the day, says Lumley, teemed with descriptions of wild scenes of "crushing, crowding, squeezing"; of ladies fainting in the press, and even of "gentlemen carried out senseless; of torn dresses and evening coats reduced to rags." Whatever opera was produced, the choice seemed to be a matter of comparative insignificance so long as the great star but appeared upon the horizon.

To Jenny Lind, says Lumley, further, the nobility and gentry and even the clergy of England—"even" is good—"offered their respectful homage and opened their country houses; Jenny Lind, the practical and living heroine of domestic drama, the prolific dispenser of world-wide charities, of whose private life every detail was caught up and diffused far and wide, with as much interest as was every trait connected with her world-wide career." Truly the way was smoothed in advance for Barnum, noble and distinguished as was his achievement.

And, of course, the way had been smoothed still earlier by her success on the Continent and by the homage of all the great, from Schumann and Mendelssohn and Meyerbeer down through all the musical notables of the time. Mendelssohn declared her to be "one of the greatest artists who ever lived and the greatest I know." He wished to write an opera for her on "The Tempest"; and such an offer was in fact announced in London, though the opera was never written, nor any other, by him. Meyerbeer discovered her in Paris when she was laboring with Manuel Garcia to restore an organ worn by faulty method and overworked, and to develop what the great singing master described as "a naturally harsh and unbending voice." But Meyerbeer does not seem to have realized then what she might become. Not till she emerged from second-class parts in the Berlin Opera did she make her first "sensation."

There have been but few discordant voices in Europe pitted against the paeans of Jenny Lind's praise; but there have been a few. One of the most notable was that of Henry F. Chorley, one of the leading English critics of the day. He was evidently stroked the wrong way by the activities of the press agent who prepared for her advent in England, and speaks of them with sarcasm, not to say with scorn. He mentions the "details of private life and authentications of private virtue as if they were not of necessity assumed — since private life and private virtue do not bare their modesty and their secrets to the paragraph maker." As to "the herald trumpets" of charities done, he observed that great singers from time immemorial had given out of both hands, regarding themselves too little; and that "the recommendation of any single singer as Charity incarnate was cruelly unjust to a hundred others."

Nevertheless, it seems to be capable of statistical proof that no other artist, up to that time, at least, unless perhaps Liszt, had given so freely, so largely in amount, or so large a proportion of an income, as Jenny Lind.

Chorley was no great admirer of her acting in operatic parts. In the "exciting scene of the first entry of Alice in 'Robert le Diable,'" the opera in which she first appeared in England, he had never seen any one so composed as Mlle. Lind was. "Her hand, even amid the thunder of applause, did not tremble — one even arranged a ring on the finger of the other." The absence of even the semblance of emotion in the midst of such overcoming excitement seemed to him strange. But he was in a minority. "Woe to those during that season who ventured to say or to write that any other great singer had ever sung in the Haymarket Opera House! They were consigned to such ignominy as belongs to the idiotic slanderer." Old friendships were broken forever: and "it was a curious experience to sit and wonder whether it really was the case that music had never been heard till the year 1847." No one would suffer the chorus of idolatry to be for a moment interrupted by any discussion of her genius and talent as compared with those of any former singer. In his book, "Thirty Years' Musical Recollections," he says, writing after the first *furore* had passed, "It can now without treason be recorded that the lower and upper half of her register were of two distinct qualities. The former was not strong, veiled, if not husky, and apt to be out of tune," an impression shared by some others. The latter was "rich, brilliant, and powerful — finest in its highest portions." He praises highly her power of respiration, her "very long breath." Her execution was great. She could use her pianissimo tones so as to make them resemble an effect of ventriloquism. In everything she did, "the skilled and careful musician was to be detected."

Chorley could not share, except at intervals, the public impression that in operatic acting she was the possessor of deep and true feeling. Many of her effects, he says, appeared over-calculated. Her Norma he found "pale and weak." Her Alice in "Robert le Diable" was excellent throughout. Her Amina in "La Sonnambula" was the part in which she made the most effect on the public. In "Lucia" her madness was "fearfully touching." Though she was extolled as an incomparable Mozart singer, Chorley considered her Susanna "stiff, heavy, conscientious." He quotes Mendelssohn as saying, "I cannot think why she always prefers to be in a bad theatre," adding after a moment's pause, "and she sings bad music the best, which is odd!" It is lamentable to read that Chorley thought Jenny Lind's sole ambition was to be the advertisement of herself, not the advancement of art.

As late as 1896, the late H. E. Krehbiel of New York experienced the force of her influence in England. In his book, "How to Listen to Music," there is a paragraph stating that Jenny Lind would brook no rivalry on the stage, and carried her jealousy to the extreme of demanding that a large portion, if not the whole, of the part of Isabella be cut out of the opera of "Robert le Diable," when she sang in it. The English publisher positively refused to accept the book for publication in England unless this paragraph, obnoxious though true, were cut out. As Mr. Krehbiel set no particular store by it, he replaced it with other matter of equal length, and the book appeared in England without wounding susceptible memories of Jenny Lind.

Jenny Lind's retirement from opera to devote herself entirely to concert and oratorio singing was generally attributed to her growing conscientious scruples against the stage and its wickedness. Mr. Chorley is mean enough to say that her operatic repertory was limited and its limitations must have exposed her to comparisons on every side, should she have remained on the stage till enthusiasm cooled. "If she became aware of this, and if such conviction had its part in her determination to give up the theatre for the concert room, the conviction was a wise one."

Her triumphs, that will stamp her name in the "Golden Book of Singers," in Chorley's estimation, were the "wild, queer northern tunes that she brought to England"—Chorley, it will be seen, does not speak as a folk-lorist—her careful expression of some of Mozart's great airs, her mastery over such a piece of execution as the Bird Song in Haydn's "Creation," the grandeur of inspiration with which she led the "Sanctus" in "Elijah."

Not everybody found her agreeable in private intercourse. Eduard Hanslick tells of a visit he made to her in Wimbledon, near London, to dine. He found her seated on a sofa under a marble bust of Queen Victoria. After a pause she asked him dryly: "Have you heard any music in London?" "Yes," answered the Viennese critic, "I had the good fortune to hear you in 'The Creation.'" A dark look came over her face and she replied, "Be so good as to leave my personality entirely out of account," in a tone of voice that chilled the listener's spine. He may have thought, if he could have collected his thoughts, that she had seen a great light or experienced a change of heart since those halcyon and vociferous days with Lumley and Barnum. Hanslick adds that her husband, Otto Goldschmidt, seemed uneasy about her manner,—or perhaps it was her manners,—and took occasion to whisper excuses for her. Later she "loosened up" enough to deliver some severe comments on the singers of the day— this was in 1862; and it may be recalled that among the singers of that day was Adelina Patti: "Present day singers all lose their voices at 30 years of age; they have studied so little and scream so much. I myself never had much voice, but I have kept it intact: indeed, I sing now with much less effort than formerly." "At home," she concluded, "I never sing a note, for I am a housewife and work like a dog." No wonder Mr. Goldschmidt was a little nervous on this occasion.

But she continued to sing in public too long. Hanslick says of that performance in "The Creation" about which she gave him such a cold douche, that the voice was like a half-effaced picture, hardly to be recognized. The tones came out veiled and weak; in the high and powerful passages with effort. A single silvery tone occasionally shot like a ray of sunshine through the gray cloud, quickly to dis-

appear. But the public applauded and gave her no
inkling that her voice was gone. Her last appearance was at a charity concert in 1883; and her death
came in 1887.

"ADELINA PATTI," the New York correspondent of *Dwight's Journal of Music* reports, in June, 1859, "is preparing for the stage, and will appear next fall, under the supervision of Strakosch, who is her brother-in-law." Her friends confidently expect, it is stated, that she will become a "really great operatic artist." For once, the admiring circle was not disappointed; nor were the newspaper critics false prophets who recorded her appearance in the Academy of Music, New York, on November 24, 1859, when she was sixteen years old. Strange to say, there was also, for once, a precocious musician about whose age and precocity there was little prevarication. It is not always that so much confidence is so fully rewarded, or that newspaper critics are so completely justified in their prophecies as those who heard her first performance as Lucia, in Donizetti's opera. It was an extraordinary success, made without the elaborate preparations of the press agent. The writers of the daily newspapers were full of enthusiasm. W. H. Fry, of *The Tribune*, considered Adelina already the equal of Sontag. He found that she "possessed unequivocally all the qualities for the rôle of Lucia," which he considered to be "a full soprano voice with absolute facility in the upper notes, thorough volatility of tone or rapid execution, great power of holding tones, especially attenuating them to the last degree, a gentle, ladylike demeanor and, to some extent, clearness of dramatic action. . . . The brilliant execution which she begins with at the outset of her career ranks with that where the best singers end." As a determined champion of American art and artists he drew the moral that "managers here make a great mistake when they fail to afford every opportunity to American aspiration, in whatever artistic form"; and claimed Adelina as "an American without a transatlantic puff, a child brought up in the midst of us." The New York correspondent of *Dwight's Journal of Music*, published in Boston, declared that the occasion " made him leap for joy, like a young hart upon the mountain "; and that since the days of Parodi there had been no such sensation as that made by "the little Patti." He then made the prediction that "there is no reason why, in ten years, Adelina Patti will not be the greatest of living singers. I wish I was as sure of $10,000 as I am of this fact." The only dubious voice in New York that has come down from the days of Patti's début is that of Richard Grant White, writing twenty-two years later, in 1881. He thought, then, that at her début she was not, even in vocalization, a "prima donna"; her voice lacked amplitude, richness, power, and her manner, though not awkward or constrained, was that of a very young girl. But "her capabilities were at once recognized by her audiences; and her future was foretold by her critics"; although, Mr. White adds, "musical criticism in New York at that time was fallen very much below the point at which it stood five years before, and that to which it has risen since."

After numerous other appearances in New York at that time, Adelina then went to Boston with the company of which she was so brilliant an ornament. The critical state of mind she met with there was one that has persisted ever since and was, no doubt, existent long before her arrival. An artistic magnificence that New York was the first to recognize must be "let down" in Boston, and must be shown to be not all that those excitable and less judicious New Yorkers had thought. Any artistic magnificence desiring unrestrained admiration in Boston should shed its effulgence first in that sober and experienced town. So we find that John S. Dwight, while he was not disappointed in "the newly famous Adelina Patti—little Patti," was prepared to be judicious in his *Journal of Music*. "A young girl, a mere child in appearance, slender, dark, and beautiful, a delicate copy of her sister, Mme. Strakosch, with all the simplicity and natural enthusiasm of a child, she sang and even acted the part of Lucy with an ease, a truthfulness, and an artistic finish that astounded and delighted every one and suggested very high comparisons. That she sings as well as Lind and Bosio and Sontag is, of course, one of the extravaganzas of the New York critics, proving, however, the real enthusiasm she created." But in his analysis of her singing he almost forgets to be an example to the extravagant New Yorkers. After delighting in the purity and beauty of her voice, its even development from the highest tones to "good, positive low tones of passion," he concludes that "she seems really destined for an artist. . . . Her execution is certainly most wonderful for one so young—so perfect you continually forget to think it strange." In her succeeding appearances the first impression was "more than confirmed." "Never were the melodies of Bellini in 'La Sonnambula' never could they be, wedded to a fresher, purer voice, in the person of a more fitting and more charming interpreter than 'little Patti.'" Of "the beauty of her rare voice, of her good vocal schooling and her singularly perfect execution" there could be no question. But the best thing about it was that "good sense, the instinct of propriety" pervaded her whole performance. The only pause to these paeans of praise was given by her singing, in a Sunday concert, of "With Verdure Clad" from "The Creation" and "Hear ye, Israel," from "Elijah"—and certainly her attempting the latter would not have been fortunate at any part of her career.

Louis Moreau Gottschalk, the American pianist, with whom Patti made a short tour of the West Indies in 1856, before her operatic début, has left in his book, "Notes of a Pianist," some interesting remarks about Adelina's family, which included an extraordinary number of fine artists: what he calls "a dynasty of distinguished singers." The father, Salvatore, was an "excellent tenore di forza." His wife, Caterina, mother of Adelina, (whose first husband was one Barili), was in 1863, when Gottschalk wrote, "still celebrated in Spain, Portugal, and Naples as a 'fiery actress,'" who sometimes had transports not connected with her art, and denounced violently audiences that did not listen with all the attention and respect she considered due her and her art. She had lived in New York for a number of years. Ireland, in his "Records of the New York Stage," mentions her début there as Romeo in Bellini's opera of "I Capuleti ed i Montecchi" (in which the hero's part is written for a soprano). He calls her "a vocalist and actress of great skill and accomplishment" but, he adds, "with advancing years and failing voice, her undoubted merits were insufficient to keep her permanently before the public." Her eldest daughter, Clotilde Barili, was successful as a singer: "young, pretty, and interesting," says Ireland, "and, for a short period, regarded as little less than a divinity by the dilettanti of New York." Ettore Barili was a baritone singer and a composer who, at one time, had a name as a fashionable teacher in New York. Nicolò, basso cantante, was "a tolerable opera singer," according to Gottschalk. Antonio, a basso profundo, was also a fashionable singing teacher; and, according to Richard Grant White, "an excellent master."

The children of the second marriage, with Salvatore Patti, raised the line to a higher eminence. Amalia, who married Maurice Strakosch, was a talented singer. She made her début in New York in 1847, as Agnise in Bellini's "Beatrice di Tenda," in which her half-sister, Clotilde, took the chief part. But her powers unfortunately deserted her before she was ready to end her career. Carlotta Patti was hardly less gifted than her famous sister Adelina. She had, as Adelina herself avowed, a higher voice. Many believed that she had a deeper feeling and a finer artistic endowment. She was originally intended for a pianist; after she became a singer her lameness prevented her from appearing in opera, unless occasionally as the Queen of the Night in Mozart's "Magic Flute," where that character has little to do but stand still and sing excruciatingly high passages of surpassing difficulty. Carlo Patti, whose resemblance to his sister Adelina, Gottschalk declares, made them "like two peas in a pod," was a fine violinist; he studied with Arditi and became the leader of the New Orleans opera orchestra, and afterwards functioned in New York and St. Louis. Gottschalk calls him a "Bohemian," who had many adventures in Calfornia and Mexico and the Southern States; and as a soldier in the Confederate Army was several times reported killed, but survived all the reports.

It is a well-known story that Adelina was born in Madrid the night after her mother had appeared there in the part of Norma. The little girl was a true child of the theatre. She resorted to it as a little girl often with her mother in their life in

Adelina Patti in America

New York and spent much time in it. The house of her brother-in-law, Maurice Strakosch, was a rendezvous for all the operatic artists who visited New York. Among them Mmes. Sontag and Alboni indulged in glowing predictions for the little girl's future. Everybody who knew her concurred with those views.

The Patti family, according to Max Maretzek, an operatic manager of that day, as he writes in his book of reminiscences, "Sharps and Flats," occupied the "humble dwelling house," No. 96, East Tenth Street; the family at home then consisting of Salvatore Patti, his wife, three daughters, Amalia, Carlotta, and Adelina, and one son, Carlo. The Maretzeks lived in the next house. Salvatore, formerly an impresario, had gone the way of most operatic managers in those days and had failed in business. In his reduced circumstances he was engaged, from 1849 to 1852, as second tenor, and his oldest daughter, Amalia, as "comprimaria," or second soprano, at the Astor Place Opera, then under Maretzek's management. The two younger Patti girls could often be seen together with the Maretzek girls in the street, "playing, running, frolicking, skipping rope, throwing snowballs at the boys in the winter and firecrakers in the summer." "The entire Patti family were born musicians," says Maretzek, "and the three daughters were gifted with beautiful voices; but Adelina had a wonderful ear in addition to her little silvery voice and could repeat the songs of Jenny Lind and Teresa Parodi after hearing them only a few times, in perfect time and tune. Often, after returning from school or from play, did Adelina call with my younger sister at the office of the Astor Place Opera House and sing, at my request, the air of 'Ernani,' or the melodies of Jenny Lind's Swedish songs, to the astonishment and delight of the singers and other persons present; and when rewarded with half a dollar, the two girls could be seen rushing to the next apple stand or candy store and invest the money received."

Maretzek recalls that once, at the Howard Athenaeum in Boston, when Mme. Barili-Patti, the mother, sang the part of Norma, with Amalia Patti as Adalgisa, Adelina figured as one of the children of Norma. Then a little child, she insisted at the rehearsal upon singing the music with her mother and sister during the duet of "Mira, Norma"; and when, after several admonitions, she would still continue to sing, the irascible mother took her up and gave her a spanking before the eyes of the orchestra and members of the company. And he recalls, again, another performance of "Norma" at the Federal Street Theatre, in which Teresa Parodi and Amalia Patti took part; and in which the two children of Norma, Adelina being one of them, acted "so naturally" that Parodi ran off the stage, Amalia Patti fainted, and the curtain had to be dropped amidst the shouting and roaring of the audience.

Luigi Arditi, who, for many years, was the operatic conductor most closely connected with Mme. Patti's career, describes in his "Reminiscences" how he first saw her in a New York hotel, which she and her mother visited to eat the macaroni prepared there by a renowned Italian *chef*. She was "a little dark-eyed, roguish maiden with red, pursed-up lips and quick, rippling laughter," and "her determined little airs and manners then already showed plainly that she was destined to become a ruler of men." She was brought to Arditi's room to sing. He was highly amused to see the airs of importance with which the tiny songstress first selected a comfortable seat for her doll, whom she bade "listen to mamma," and then turned to him, asking him to accompany her in "Ah, non giunge," from "La Sonnambula." He and Bottesini, the famous double-bass player, who was with him, both wept "genuine tears of emotion," and were amazed at the "well-nigh perfect manner in which she delivered some of the most difficult and varied arias without the slightest effort or self-consciousness."

Richard Grant White also saw the little Patti some years before her operatic début under similar intimate and affecting circumstances, although with no tears of emotion. He was visiting Patti's mother — "a very motherly seeming woman, who showed all of her forty-five or fifty years." He observed a "slender, swarthy, bright-eyed little girl, in short skirts, who ran into the room and chirped at her mother, and ran out of it, carolling as she went through the passageway, and then ran in and out again in the same fashion," until the middle-aged prima donna with whom he was talking called out rather sharply, "Adelina, tacete! e venite a me, o andate via." The child chose to come. "Soon she left her mother's side for mine, and then with the freedom of Italian childhood . . . half sat upon my knee, swinging one red-stockinged leg as she glanced from her mother's face to mine. I asked Mme. Barili-Patti if her little daughter promised to be a singer like her sisters and her mother, to which she replied, 'Lo spero; lo credo.' And then,

Adelina Patti in America

'Cantate un poco, Adelina, per il signore,' and she suggested something, whereupon the girl, without leaving her perch, sang, like a bird, a little Italian air that I did not know and soon ran away on some childish errand."

Grant White thought that to be with her mother in itself must have been a liberal education in music; and the examples before her, night and day, the very atmosphere she breathed, tended to foster her musical talents.

According to Patti's own story, told to Eduard Hanslick, her half-brother, Ettore Barili, was her first teacher. Strakosch, she declared, only coached her as Rosina in "Il Barbiere," and later, when she had begun her career in Europe, in her other parts. He himself claimed a much greater share in her early training. But much was owed to Strakosch in other ways, if not in this. Patti's mother wished to send her to Italy as a little girl to accept an engagement there. When Strakosch, then a New York operatic manager, heard of this he protested so vigorously against the idea that it was abandoned. Adelina herself declared that at that time her voice was already on the road to ruin and had begun to show a tremolo. A season in Italy would doubtless have been the end of it.

Musical Discourse

When did Patti make her "positively first" appearance before the public? She had already sung in many concerts before her operatic début. Herman Klein, in his book, "The Reign of Patti," thinks it was at a charity concert, of which the date and details are irrevocably lost. But Ireland, in his "Records of the New York Stage," notes that at a benefit concert in Niblo's Garden, on December 3, 1851, one of the performers was "the very remarkable child, Adelina Patti, whose voice and execution were the astonishment of the town,"—she being then just under nine years of age. This was the fourth annual benefit of the American Dramatic Fund Association. Hamblin and Laura Addison appeared in "Catherine and Petruchio"; an "Italian concert" was given by Signora Borghese and Signora Steffanone, Signor Forti and Signor Vietti, and Adelina; and "the whole Ravel company" appeared in the pantomime of "Mazulme."

If Adelina's own memory served her, she made appearances in concerts in the United States—she did not say where—in 1850, when she was seven years old. They used to stand her on a table near the pianoforte that the audience, as she thought, might get a full view of her doll. Her account is that she sang "Una Voce Poco Fa" from "Il Barbiere" with the same vocal embroideries that she used later in her famous years. Were they the ones that elicited Rossini's sad sarcasm in Paris when, after one of her brilliant appearances, rendered doubly brilliant by her elaborate decorations of Rosina's melody, he asked her if it was really his music that she had been singing?

Max Maretzek, already an operatic manager in New York and a friend of Adelina's father, declares that her first public appearance was under his management in February, 1852. It was at a concert of Michael — "Miska" — Hauser, the violinist, at Tripler Hall in Broadway, who was also assisted by Teresa Parodi and Cesare Badiali, two of the noted operatic singers of the day. "Afterwards she appeared in two concerts given by her half-brother in John Brougham's Lyceum Theatre, on May 12 and June 8, 1852, on which occasions she sang the 'Echo Song' by Eckert and 'Ah, non giunge' from 'La Sonnambula.' Her success was complete, but more one of wonder than of admiration"— which, considering her age, was not strange. In 1853 Adelina made a tour with Ole Bull in the South and West of the United States. The company included, besides Ole Bull, Adelina, her sister Amalia, and Strakosch, Amalia's husband. They gave many concerts; Mrs.

Ole Bull, in her "Memoir" of her husband, says "some two hundred." There were no societies for the prevention of cruelty to children in those days. Mrs. Bull quotes from a Southern newspaper, unnamed, a flattering welcome to the "musical prodigy, only eight years old" —she was really ten—in which the writer expresses the belief that "Signora Patti will nestle herself in many a memory to-night in company with Jenny Lind and Catherine Hayes, not because she is such a singer as they are, but because her youth will impart to her performance a charm that their matured powers cannot give." In 1856 came the short tour in the West Indies with Gottschalk, above mentioned.

It is not strange, after all this, that the voice gave ominous danger-signals; and that the clear-sighted Strakosch—if indeed he had as much control over Adelina's doings as he avers—made her refrain from singing entirely for two whole years and then began to teach her, with circumspection, a few rôles. He is even said to have fought hard against her appearing at her operatic début in the Academy of Music, fearing that the theatre was too big for her voice.

After her effulgent success in the winter of 1859 and the following year in New York, Strakosch formed a partnership with her father, Salvatore Patti, to take her on a concert tour in the Western and Southern States. In January, February, and March, 1861, Adelina appeared as prima donna at the French Opera House in New Orleans, which for so many years boasted that it was the only "permanent" opera in the United States. A New Orleans chronicler mentions "Robert le Diable," "Il Trovatore," "Les Huguenots," "Lucia," "Charles VI," (by Halévy) "Le Pardon de Ploermel" (otherwise Meyerbeer's "Dinorah"), as the operas in which she appeared, to which another chronicler adds " Marta." An advertisement in January announced "Le Barbier de Séville," in the "lesson scene" of which Mlle. Patti would sing "Mme. Sontag's celebrated 'Echo Song' [*i.e.*, Eckert's] and the Scottish ballad ' Within a Mile of Edinboro' Town.'" Prices on that occasion, it may be noted, ranged from 50 cents to $1.50; the doors were opened at 6.30 o'clock and the performance began at 7. New Orleans' local pride may be read in the chronicler's declaration that "it was on the French Opera House stage that Adelina Patti scored her early successes and where her genius received the stamp of approval that made it recognized throughout the capitals of the world."

In the spring of 1861, a year and a half after her

New York début in opera, Patti went to England and began that brilliant European experience that placed her unequivocally where the prescient New York reviewers had placed her, at the head of the world's singers. Her success in London was a surprise. The English people looked on the reports of her American achievements as extravagant; and at her first appearance as Amina in "La Sonnambula," at the Royal Italian Opera, Covent Garden, not twenty people in the house knew beforehand that she possessed more than ordinary ability. The press agent had neglected his opportunity and the advertisements were silent. The surprise was "indescribable"; and confident predictions were made of a successor to Bosio, Malibran, and Pasta.

She had made a great name when she returned to America for the first time in 1881, for concert and operatic performances. In 1884 she came to sing at the Academy of Music in Colonel Mapleson's company, with which he was trying to rival the efforts of Henry E. Abbey at the newly-established Metropolitan Opera House. It was the twenty-fifth anniversary of her first appearance at the Academy. The late H. E. Krehbiel tells entertainingly, in his book, "Chapters of Opera," of the lame attempts to celebrate the anniversary — of the dragging of the diva's carriage through the streets from the Academy to the Windsor Hotel in Fifth Avenue by a perfunctory band of Italians hired for the purpose by the Colonel; of the banquet in her honor, which she cheerfully accepted, and which the wives of most of the eminent gentlemen invited positively refused to attend, on account of the then recent scandal over her separation from the Marquis de Caux, her first husband, and her marriage with the tenor Nicolini.

In 1893 she came back again for an ill-advised "farewell tour" that could add nothing to her reputation, because her powers were waning, and that caused her admirers to grieve. They grieved still more when she came again in 1903, on another "farewell tour," not a single feature of which was worthy of her and which was a baldly planned scheme to exploit the curiosity of the younger generation and the fond memories of the older. The voice in her youth was a pure high soprano; but it dropped a little in its range as she advanced in years; and in her last years a good deal. In the lamentable last "farewell tour" she had many of her arias transposed a minor third downward. Even a considerable time before this she had had to resort to transpositions. Much has been said about the wonderful preservation of Mme. Patti's voice. It was indeed wonderfully preserved, and for many years; though at the end she relied too much upon this preservation. A candid colleague and friend, Clara Louise Kellogg, the American soprano, who wrote her memoirs without hesitating to drop a little acid here and there, asks how it could have been otherwise, considering the care she took of herself and it. "Such a life! Everything divided off carefully, according to régime; so much to eat, so far to walk, so long to sleep, just such and such things to do and no others! And above all, she allowed herself no emotions." Every singer knows, observes Miss Kellogg, that emotions are what exhaust and injure the voice. "She never acted, and she never, never felt!" Miss Kellogg is kind enough to add, however, that after she had "run away with Nicolini," Mme. Patti did succeed in putting an unusual amount of warmth into the rôle of Violetta. Otherwise her acting, this contemporary continues, was essentially mechanical. "She never was at all resourceful as an actress and never able to stamp any part with the least creative individuality."

It was a part of Mme. Patti's preservative system that she never rehearsed. Her contracts stipulated that, while she should be allowed to rehearse if she wanted to, she should never be compelled to. And, as a matter of fact, she never did. It has been picturesquely asserted that Mme. Patti's whole course of life was based on the theory that she had in her throat a certain definitely limited number of notes to be expended, and that when these were gone, there would be no more. Consequently, by economizing her expenditure at rehearsals and on other unprofitable occasions, she could make her voice last so much longer.

But the laws of nature are inexorable. Mme. Patti, thanks to the perfection of her art, was able to postpone their operation longer than most singers have done; but even she could not defy them. There was certainly cause for wonder, at her appearances in New York in 1903, that she could retain and utilize in public even so much of her voice as she did; but some were fain to think, on these occasions, that wonder was not the ostensible purpose of the concerts she gave, nor the reason why the public was invited to attend at very high prices. Her appearances gave proof of what required no proof and what should never have been put to the proof—that a human voice may be less lasting than the human being who possesses it. There was not much to admire or to arouse pleasure in the singing she did, as singing. The wonder was that it was the voice of a woman within a few months of sixty-one years.

What beauty it preserved was the result of her life-long art. But she had to reach desperately for high notes, even though her arias were transposed as much as a minor third; those notes were frequently taken with faulty intonation—and that by a singer whose ear in her prime had never let her lose the pitch by a hair's breadth; her runs and arpeggios were dull and uncertain; her trills were subdued and promptly cut off; her phrasing was short and disjointed, showing failure of breath; the production of tone was not seldom perilously near to ugliness.

There are numerous stories of Mme. Patti's relentless pursuit of the dollar in America, as well as of other financial units in other countries. It was only too evident that this last "farewell" was a final attempt to capitalize her enormous reputation and to wrest what there was left to gain from it. There were rather sordid little details for helping to this end. Thus, it was clearly put down in her contract that she should appear twice upon all the programmes and no more, and that she should deliver one and only one encore after her first piece and two, and no more, after the other. The pieces, as well as the encores, all drawn from a very limited repertory, were all enumerated and printed in the programme-books of the concerts. The most degrading feature of it all was the contract, entered into with a certain popular song writer of the Broadway school for the purpose of advertising his wares, that Mme. Patti should sing, as an encore at each of her concerts, a deplorably tasteless production of his own in which the cheapness of the words vied with the vulgarity of the music. It was a pitiable thing that so great an artist should end her career in the city where she began it, in such a way as this. And, from one point of view, the worst of it was that she did not really need the money.

The result of this last tour in America was disastrous for the singer's manager and his backers, as other tours of hers had been. It was not at all disastrous for her: she took back with her to Craig-y-Nos some $200,000. At her last appearance in New York the audience was productive of only $3,180 and the manager was slow in depositing in her hands the $5,000 without which, in plain sight, for each appearance, she invariably refused to stir. She waited placidly in her hotel, the audience waited impatiently in the theatre. The manager distractedly ran about town to secure from his principals the $2,000 that were lacking. These gentlemen were said to be too overcome to speak to reporters about it; but the concert went on and the audience was appeased. It was by no means Mme. Patti's first experience of the kind; she had learned wisdom by experience. Nor was it her last. Many of the final appearances in different parts of the country, especially the Southwest, that were to close her tour, were cancelled because the audiences were not such as were hoped for, in numbers. The projector of this last farewell lost $25,000. Probably he deserved to.

The ideals that Mme. Patti represented are notably divergent from those of the present day. The happy-go-lucky representations of opera, such as Colonel Mapleson gave at the Academy of Music in New York for so many years, were for her the sum of operatic art. Opera-goers were not then so insistent as they have since come to be upon dramatic verity, upon finish and completeness of ensemble, upon good orchestral playing, upon the artistic whole of an operatic performance. They wanted the voices of great singers; and they got them. How much is it owing to the dearth of great singers that a different ideal has now come to prevail?

It would lead a long way to discuss the question why really great voices, or really great vocal art, such as Mme. Patti's, are no longer in evidence. Conditions in modern life and art, especially in the operatic business, prevent their development and perfect flowering. The efforts of a younger generation to believe that the methods and results of various modern singers, all more or less raw and in different degrees unfinished and imperfect, really represent the artistic line and traditions of a Patti, are pathetic; and what corroboration the younger gets from an older generation denotes either a failure of memory or a lack of knowledge. Such ideals as Mme. Patti represented, so far as they relate purely to vocal art, are precious; and their loss or neglect necessarily involves the ultimate destruction of good singing. So far as they represent carelessness or indifference toward dramatic values and artistic finish in the lyric drama, they are superseded, and happily so. But the loss is a sore one, which nothing else of a different sort can ever quite make up for.

FRANZ KNEISEL

FRANZ KNEISEL had achieved a full and richly rounded career in America, although when he died in New York on March 26, 1926, he was hardly at the threshold of old age. His was a character and a personality and a musical nature that exactly fitted him to do what he set out to do. He had an iron will, an unyielding determination. He had been given the finest training that Vienna in the early eighties, still preserving the greatest of musical traditions, could afford. Like all who have reached high places in the art of music, he was precocious; though he was not an "infant prodigy" and was never exploited as one. To be, when not yet out of his 'teens, concert master of the Hofburg Theatre in Vienna—though, to be sure, that was not one of the most responsible of musical positions—then, as successor to Ysaye and César Thomson, concert-master of Bilse's orchestra in Berlin, a famous organization in its day; and then to be summoned in his twentieth year to occupy the same place in the newly formed Boston Symphony Orchestra—all this is a record that means much.

The Boston Symphony Orchestra was entering the fourth year of its existence in the autumn of 1885 when Kneisel joined it. Gericke had been appointed conductor, succeeding Georg Henschel, and

Franz Kneisel

had found it necessary to make a good many changes
in the *personnel* of the orchestra, which had been at
first constituted of resident Boston musicians, young
and old. Too many of them were old, as well as incompetent, and their title to places in the orchestra
was read more in the records of honorable careers
than in present achievement. Boston was angry and
excited over Major Higginson's ambitious attempt
to found a new orchestra and his determination to
support his conductor in importing young musicians of talent to assure its competence. Mr. Kneisel
as a youth succeeded the veteran Bernhard Listemann as concert-master. There was bitter comment. One newspaper critic voiced a widespread
feeling when he wrote: "To drop Mr. Listemann
from the position of concert master seems almost as
terrific as it would be to discharge Mr. Zerrahn from
the directorship of the Handel and Haydn." Could
a more terrific comparison be made? Some insisted
that the importation of Mr. Kneisel and other
young violinists from abroad was an insult to America as well as to Boston; for the first duty of an established orchestra was to encourage American composers and to benefit local musicians. The youth of
Mr. Kneisel and the others—about a score of them,
there were—was an additional cause of irritation.

The new concert-master was one of the youngest of them — "so young," said Mr. Gericke, in recalling those days long afterwards, "that he did not even know how to smoke. On our trip over I felt it my duty to teach him this art, in which he has certainly been a past master ever since."

Mr. Kneisel began his duties as concert-master on October 17, 1885. On October 31 he made his first appearance with the orchestra as a soloist, playing Beethoven's violin concerto. Criticism was ready to be launched: "He showed only a moderate force; his manner had none of Mr. Listemann's life or nervous energy." He was "a quiet, simple player." One of the most critical as well as distinguished members of the orchestra was heard to remark to his neighbor after the first movement: "Der Kerl spielt schön" — the fellow plays beautifully. There was very soon a realization among the members of the orchestra that this "Kerl" was a person of power and distinction. The realization spread in due course to the critics and the public. He stood for a discipline in the orchestral rehearsals — seconding, of course, Mr. Gericke's determination — that was then uncommon; and in many ways showed himself to be a concert-master of a sort that till then had hardly been known here.

Franz Kneisel

Mr. Kneisel's first experiences as concert-master were of a kind to require a certain circumspection. He was, of course, aware of the suspicion, not to say the hostility, in at least certain quarters, with which he was viewed as a new-comer and a supplanter of an old favorite. He was resolved that there should be no blunders or lapses so far as he could prevent them. One of his first precautions was characteristic. On the first programme of the season stood Weber's "Oberon" overture. To make certain that the new contingent of young men should do themselves credit at the first concert, he summoned them all before the first rehearsal to his own rooms where they practised together the brilliant violin passages, so that they should be sure of making the most striking effect; and that was the result at the concert. Indeed, the brilliancy, warmth, and precision of the violins of the Boston Symphony Orchestra were for many years among the chief glories of the organization, that contributed most largely to its fame. Many people can still remember the first concert of the Boston Symphony Orchestra in New York, when this same "Oberon" overture began the programme. It was by no means an unfamiliar thing to the New York audience; but the effect of the performance was unusual from its fire and sweep. Staid music-lovers, brought up on immemorial years of the Philharmonic Society, stood up—some, it is said, on the seats—cheering and waving handkerchiefs.

Mr. Kneisel once summed up his conception of the concert-master somewhat as follows:

"The concert-master is, in a way, the autocratic conductor's grand vizier, his executive officer, his chief means of making effective his wishes, and, where the right relationship exists, his best friend and right-hand man. His functions resemble those of a constitutional monarch's prime minister. The king can do no wrong. If all goes well in the orchestra, it is the conductor's merit; if anything goes amiss, it is very likely to be the concert-master's fault. He must always see that all the instruments are in tune with one another before rehearsals and concerts begin. In most cases he sees that the violin, and perhaps the other string parts, are properly marked for bowing and phrasing, which he determines himself, in order that all shall play alike— though not always is uniformity of bowing considered indispensable. If there is a misunderstanding between the conductor and any player, the concert-master's good offices are invaluable in setting it right. He advises the conductor as to the deficiencies or excellences of individual players, and may often

be called upon to assist in engaging new men. If
the conductor makes a mistake—and even the
greatest conductor sometimes does—the concert-
master is there to see that the force of it is broken
in some way. Few conductors are familiar with all
the details of technique and the limitations and
possibilities of all the orchestral instruments; and
if the conductor gives a direction as to phrasing
or accent that is impracticable, the concert-master
must be ready after the rehearsal to explain to the
bewildered or derisive player that something else
was really meant, and also to intimate to the mistaken autocrat that some modification of his desires
had better be made. In case of direst need, should
conductor and orchestra get into trouble in a public performance, the concert-master must, if he can,
bring them together again with the sound of his
instrument, more potent at such a moment than
the conductor's stick. Or should a soloist miss a cue
or make a false entrance he must, if possible, give
such a hint or catch up such a missing strand as
shall set the unlucky one aright."

These are counsels of perfection, and it should
be said that all conductors will not often need all
or much of this kind of aid; nor will all concert-
masters be able to give it. But, such a concert-

master will be invaluable to any conductor and is of importance to the prosperity of the orchestra only less than the conductor himself. It is rather the fashion nowadays to belittle the importance of the concert-master as a result in the growth of the artistic position and prominence of the conductor; and, perhaps, also of his capacity and knowledge. But that is the sort of concert-master Franz Kneisel was; and for the period of his service with the Boston Symphony Orchestra he was a tower of strength to it. There have been, perhaps, few in his position who have had so much influence and authority, so much knowledge, so much presence of mind and skill in the duties of his office as he.

It was part of Mr. Higginson's plan to found a first-rate string quartet in Boston as well as a first-rate orchestra, and the coming of Mr. Kneisel and the other "young lions of the Conservatoire," as Berlioz called another and similar group in Paris, gave the opportunity for it. Mr. Higginson established it, and bore it on his shoulders, as he did the orchestra, for some years. The Kneisel Quartet gave its first concert in Boston in the old Chickering Hall on December 28, 1885. There had, of course, been chamber music before that in Boston. The Mendelssohn Quintette Club had fought a long, brave fight to make chamber music popular, and had made a name for itself. There were other chamber music organizations. But the audiences were small and the fight was against odds. The new-comers showed that there was a new spirit and a new standard set, and there was an increase in the public's interest in this form of music. The programme of the first concert was this: Volkmann's quartet in G minor, Op. 14; the canzonetta from Mendelssohn's quartet in E flat; the menuetto from Mozart's quartet in C minor and Beethoven's quintet in C, Op. 29; not an exacting demand upon an untried audience. The Quartet was then made up of Messrs. Kneisel, Fiedler, Svecenski and Giese; Daniel Kunz played the second viola in the quintet. There were four concerts in Boston in the first season. They began at 7.45 o'clock.

The first concert in New York took place in Steinway Hall on March 11, 1888, assisted by Conrad Ansorge, at that time a noted pianist. The programme included Schubert's posthumous quartet in D Minor, Rubinstein's trio in B flat, Op. 52, and Schumann's quartet in A, Op. 41, No. 3. The Kneisel Quartet gave no more concerts in New York till they undertook a series of four in the season of 1891–92. These took place in the ballroom of Sherry's old

establishment in Fifth Avenue at Thirty-seventh
Street. The first of these was notable as giving the
first American performance of Brahms's quintet,
Op. 111. The organization was then composed of
Messrs. Kneisel, Roth, Svecenski and Schroeder,
and had the assistance in the quintet of Ottokar
Novacek, viola. The other numbers of the pro-
gramme consisted of Mozart's quartet in C and
Tchaikovsky's in D.

There was a hard row to hoe in getting established in New York. After a time Mr. Kneisel was
on the point of giving up his New York concerts;
but the persuasion of a few ardent lovers of chamber music prevailed, and induced another trial. The
turning-point came and the public thereafter gave
an increasingly firm and unwavering support to the
organization, which continued to the end. The end
came in April, 1917, when, to the dismay of his
admirers in New York and all over the country,
Mr. Kneisel disbanded his Quartet. In a communi-
cation to his subscribers he said:

"The desire that the high standard which has
been before us from the beginning should not be
permitted to suffer depreciation has of late years
been a cause of great concern to me; and the responsibility has become a burden—so great a bur-

den, indeed, that I have reluctantly come to the decision to end the career of the Kneisel Quartet with the last concert of this season."

Once before the Kneisel Quartet had been in danger of dissolution. In 1907 negotiations were opened between Mr. Kneisel and the committee of the Philadelphia Orchestra, after the death of Fritz Scheel, to secure him as conductor of that organization. Kneisel had had experience in conducting as a substitute for the conductor of the Boston Orchestra on many occasions, and his powers and experience were such as to insure his success in Philadelphia. Another consideration that urged him to accept the offer from Philadelphia was the resignation of Alwin Schroeder, 'cellist of the Quartet, who wished to return to Germany to live. This would involve for Kneisel a trip to Europe to find his successor, and a summer of hard rehearsal to "break him in" when found. An agreement with the orchestral authorities was almost concluded, but Kneisel was dissuaded in time by his New York friends, and the Kneisel Quartet was saved for ten years more of activity. Kneisel had before this left the post of concert-master of the Boston Orchestra and had transferred his home and that of his quartet to New York, in 1903, to devote all his time to quartet playing and, with the members of the organization, to establishing and carrying on the department of string teaching in the newly founded Institute of Musical Art in that city. Here he developed great qualities as a teacher and made the institution, of which he was so important a part, among the finest in this country.

It was as a quartet player that Kneisel made his greatest achievements and his most important contribution to American musical culture. Such performances as he offered were a new revelation in this country, where quartet playing, before his time, had generally been a by-product, the result of orchestral players' leisure moments. With him it was, even from the first, a chief end. He spent upon it an enormous amount of time and labor in rehearsal, of thought, knowledge, mastery of style, and infinite attention to detail. He had an unequalled acquaintance with the literature and appreciation of diverse styles of chamber music. He never brought forward in public performance any work, new or old, until he had become thoroughly imbued with its spirit and possessed of a mastery of its outward form and technical difficulties. This meant, sometimes, years of ripening by reflection, experiment, and repetition. A fruit of such methods was his per-

Franz Kneisel

formance of the last five string quartets of Beethoven, for so long a sealed book to players and listeners alike. It is not too much to say that he first made them truly known to American audiences, not only by mastering their technical difficulties in the matter of ensemble and perfect coördination, but also by penetrating their recondite spirit and laying it bare to comprehending listeners.

Kneisel believed it his duty to set before his public all the best of what was "modern" in the years of his activity. There was weeping and gnashing of teeth, sometimes, among his subscribers; but he never gave way when he thought there was something to be played that was worthy of attention. And many of the works thus forcibly fed by him to his public have since been accepted as a living part of the modern repertory. An interesting episode was his playing of the "American" quartet and quintet of Dvořák, who was then living in New York, fresh from the composer's hand — "die Tinte noch nass" — and in the composer's presence. He knew Brahms in his summer abode near Ischl in Austria, went there in his own vacations with his quartet, and played Brahms's and other chamber music with him and for him. The result was an authority in these works that few others could claim.

What Brahms mostly wished to hear from him, besides his own works, was Haydn; Beethoven's quartets, he said, you hear from all quarters. But Brahms never but once made any suggestions to Kneisel as to changing the tempo he had taken, or the conception he had set forth — various artists have testified to his toleration of competent musicians, intelligent and sympathetic; even, in the case of singers, to the extent of allowing changes in the melodic line, if it was too high for them. The one criticism that Brahms made of a performance in which Kneisel participated was made in a characteristic way. Mr. Kneisel had played with a certain noted woman pianist Brahms's G minor pianoforte quartet, following, much against his will, the lady's tempo in the Andante and its intermediate Animato, which he felt to be much too slow and too fast, respectively. Brahms, when it was finished, took up a pencil and went to the pianist's score with the remark: "Ah, I see I was mistaken — I should have written 'Adagio' and 'Presto' over those movements"; and he did so. Among other things Kneisel played him César Franck's string quartet, which was then hardly known outside of France. He listened in complete silence, and when it was done, spoke not one word of comment.

Franz Kneisel

Kneisel's work as a teacher was carried on from his earlier years; and after 1917 absorbed all his time and attention. His work at the Institute of Musical Art in New York was continued in the summers at Blue Hill, Maine, whither a score of favored pupils followed him year after year and were subjected to the same kind of intensive discipline that prevailed between them in the winter. Hard work was a necessity for him, rest a rare luxury. But when he did rest he knew how to discharge his mind of all preoccupations. He taught with love and devotion to art always uppermost, and would not waste his time on incompetent pupils. To them he recommended other occupations than music. To those whom he did teach he put artistry, true musicianship, as the end to be striven for, rather than virtuosoship. The demands he made on his pupils were severe, stringent. They involved the long look ahead. He would take as pupils only such as intended to aim at the highest things and to make a sustained and intensive effort. He left behind him no pupils who took a few lessons to announce themselves as "pupils of Kneisel." With all the severity of his discipline and of his demands upon those who studied with him, he never undertook to fashion them all after the same mould. He did not assail the individuality of his pupils, and they left him, when the time came for leaving him, as artists in their own right, not as replicas of Kneisel, or ear-marked as a set of " Kneisel pupils." What they had in common was thoroughness of grounding, high ideals of their art, a sane and intelligent and well-informed outlook upon it. In the charming little music building put up at Blue Hill, his summer home in Maine, by the interest of a devoted friend, he taught ensemble as well as solo playing. They were golden hours of opportunity, and those who had the privilege of sharing them will always prize them as a unique privilege.

One of the things that Kneisel had nearest his heart in his later years was the Bohemian Club of musicians, in New York. He was one of its founders and its president till his death. Perhaps the continued and increasing success of this organization of a class of men who have not always been able to get on together and dwell in complete harmony— the "irritabile genus" of professional musicians— tells much about the most delightful and beguiling sides of his character.

There have been few men who have done as much for the musical culture of his adopted country as Franz Kneisel. As concert-master, quartet leader—

Franz Kneisel

making not only the greatest organization of its kind in this country, but also one that could bear comparison with the best and most famous in the world—and as teacher of the finest fibre who bestowed upon his pupils the inestimable gift of musicianship rather than virtuosoship, his great service was in the new standards he set, the new revelations he made. This was especially true as to chamber music. Here his genius found fullest scope; for this task his peculiar qualities of musicianship fitted him preëminently. He may be said to have been the first to show in this country what could be achieved in chamber music by high technical mastery, unlimited work in rehearsal, the ripening of sometimes years of thought and reflection, joined to deep musical insight, wide sympathies, unquestioned authority, an unerring taste, and intuitive musical feeling. Genius is by no means to be summed up as the taking of infinite pains; but genius such as Kneisel's reached its highest manifestations along that path. No labor, no effort, was ever too great for him; and the results are writ large in the record he left. For what he did this country owes him a debt of gratitude that will not soon be forgotten.

HENRY EDWARD KREHBIEL

A GREAT personality and a great force passed away from the musical life of the United States in the death, on March 20, 1923, at the age of sixty-nine years, of Henry Edward Krehbiel, "dean," as he was affectionately known, of American musical critics. His New York colleagues united in doing honor to his memory in their city the day after his death, and there were appreciative notices of him in the London press. Not one but had some peculiar personal tribute to the impression of greatness that he had made. Krehbiel, indeed, had a place in America that corresponded to that of the great critics of the nineteenth century in Europe; a place of commanding influence and authority. He had put the profession of musical criticism upon a higher plane of knowledge and competence in all that makes for a true basis of judgment, than it had ever occupied in America before his day. The fifty years that he spent in the exercise of it saw a great advance in the numbers of the musical public in the United States, a great elevation in the standard of taste and knowledge. To this Krehbiel had contributed more than one man's share. Not only by his daily preachments in his newspaper, *The New York Tribune*, but also by a five-foot shelf of books on various aspects of

Henry Edward Krehbiel

musical art, he wrought for better things and higher standards, for the prevalence of artistic rectitude and a true understanding.

What he did came from a great critical faculty, a deep comprehension of his subject. The soundness and discrimination of his judgment were based on a profound knowledge of the history of music, an acquaintance with all the developments of the art since its beginnings, a familiarity with its technical ramifications, a knowledge of schools and their spirit. But all this great learning was always put at the service of the present. He was no historical grubber for the sake of grubbing. What he knew entered into the fibre of his critical faculty and helped him in the understanding and appreciation of the new, in the piercing of fraud and futility and feebleness. True scholar that he was, he was a graduate of no university. He had the culture of an intellect that could assimilate the best and that was eager to do so, that was the fruit of wide reading and delight in literature; a culture not always brought away from the university. And this culture always underlay his writing and shone through it.

Krehbiel was born in Ann Arbor, Michigan, March 10, 1854, the son of a German-American Methodist clergyman. He was in his earliest youth a student in a law office; but not for long. He could hardly have imbibed there much more than the elementary principles of the law, but he always, to the end of his life, prided himself a little on this legal lore that lay at the bottom of his mind; and now and again it would make itself felt and come to the surface in some surprising way. He was soon graduated from law to journalism. His earliest work in that way was on *The Cincinnati Gazette*, where he won a place as a "star" reporter. One of his accomplishments was the reporting of baseball; and he always prided himself a little on a new way of baseball scoring, which he claimed to have invented. As a general reporter he had many interesting and some grewsome experiences. One of the stories that he sometimes told was of helping a much-distressed gentleman in tracing the body of his father, which in some unknown way had disappeared soon after his death. They went on many a mysterious and forbidding round in Cincinnati's purlieus; and the body was finally found in the dissecting room of a medical school. The distressed gentleman was Benjamin Harrison, afterwards President of the United States, and the body was that of the son of another President of the United States. There were famous murder cases which Krehbiel had to report in Cincinnati. In some

of the strange adventures that fell to the lot of a
"star" reporter he made the acquaintance of Lafcadio
Hearn, who was then a "word painter" on one
of the rival newspapers, preparing for his later literary
career; and they were friends. Hearn had a
literary interest in music and in some of his later
explorations in the West Indies collected some folk-
songs that he sent to add to Krehbiel's collections.
The breaking of their friendship was an extraordinary
incident, characteristic of the eccentric and
high-strung nature of Hearn. After Krehbiel had
come to New York to live, Hearn one day called upon
him. Going away, he forgot his rubbers and came
back to get them. The maid who opened the door,
and who had not seen him before, was so alarmed at
his extraordinary appearance that she refused to let
him in. Hearn went off in a rage, accusing Krehbiel
of appropriating his rubbers; and their friendship,
notwithstanding efforts to repair it, was broken.

After he had come to New York at the invitation
of Whitelaw Reid, Editor of *The New York Tribune*,
who himself had made his journalistic beginnings
on *The Cincinnati Gazette*, John R. G. Hassard,
musical critic of *The Tribune*, did not at once let
go entirely of the business of musical criticism; and
Krehbiel had much "general work" to do. He had

such jobs as "covering" the wreck of a steamer off Marthas Vineyard, that meant some uncomfortable adventures along the Massachusetts coast. He regularly sat at the desk of the night city editor on the incumbent's "night off." He was successful in interviewing public men; and some of his achievements with Thurlow Weed, at that time the ruler of the Republican party at Albany, with Jay Gould, and other difficult "subjects," are remembered by old newspaper men. For many years after he had gained prominence as *The Tribune's* musical critic, he was sent to "cover" the annual boat races of the college crews at New London and Poughkeepsie, in June. One of his regular summer "jobs" was to take the place, on his vacation, of one of the subordinate editorial writers in *The Tribune* office, whose task was to write short editorial paragraphs intended to comment on the news of the night that came in after the regular editorial writers had gone home.

All this is simply to emphasize the fact that Krehbiel was first and foremost a newspaper man. He esteemed journalism as a liberal profession and was incessantly jealous of its honor and high standing. He was proud of his calling as a newspaper man and proud to be known as one, proud of his experience and competence as such.

Henry Edward Krehbiel

As a critic Krehbiel had an unusual power of analyzing and penetrating to the essential quality of a musical work on a first hearing. His analyses of important new compositions from the score, before their first performance in New York, were masterly and authoritative. His discussion of such works as Tchaikovsky's sixth symphony and Dvořák's "New World" symphony and the "American" quartet and quintet of the same composer were notable contributions to his newspaper. Earlier than these his articles on the great Wagnerian music-dramas, when they were first produced at the Metropolitan Opera House in the seasons of 1884–1886, running in several issues of the newspaper, and later collected in his book, "Studies in the Wagnerian Drama," were among the authoritative essays in the Wagner literature.

Krehbiel was an early and ardent champion of Wagner, and his work did much to interpret the great music-dramas and awaken a love and understanding of them in America. His keen insight saw the value of Brahms, Tchaikovsky, Dvořák, and others of the schools that were once new, and when they were new. "'Ware the Muscovite" was his early summons to give ear to the school of the Russian nationalists, when it first appeared upon the horizon of musical art. Subsequently he did not follow the advances of the later schools, as is natural and inevitable with increasing years; and he was never an ardent admirer of Debussy, of the later Strauss, and still less of those who have troubled the surface of the musical waters since.

The preoccupation of the Russian nationalists with folk-music of their native land was one of the reasons that interested Krehbiel so strongly in their compositions. For folk-music was one of the great and enduring passions of his life. It arose in him early and continued to the end. He made many original investigations into such manifestations of it as come naturally into the ken of an American student, and he was always an ardent champion of the use of it by composers, and especially by American composers, for artistic purposes. His attention was devoted chiefly to the negro folk-tunes and "spirituals," of which he had made a large collection, and had an intimate and first-hand knowledge. His work on this subject was finally embodied in his book, "Afro-American Folk Songs," published in 1914. It was his contention that these songs are the nearest to folk-songs that America has produced or could, under modern conditions, produce; that they are truly American, as having been created here, and as giving voice to an important section of Americans; and that, while they are not the product of the dominant race, they have qualities and characteristics that make them appeal strongly to that race. He did not succeed in gaining universal acceptance of his views; but Krehbiel's preaching of folk-song, in season and out of season, had no little influence on the composers of America.

As a critic Krehbiel had a mind open to such of the newer manifestations of the art as seemed to him based on the elements of true progress, on beauty, and sincerity. As has just been suggested, he could not penetrate into certain regions that have now been accepted by many as belonging to the realms of the beautiful in art. Other and later developments were abhorrent to him. Whatever may be the right or the wrong in the matter, it was natural and inevitable that this should be so. He was above all a classicist — a lover of Bach, Mozart, Beethoven, Schubert, of the newer romantics, of the great men of the past who have erected the greatest and most enduring structures of art. Of Mozart and Beethoven he was a deep student; and on the latter, especially, a great and original authority. Of that he has left an enduring proof in his edition of

Musical Discourse

A. W. Thayer's "Life of Beethoven." The third and last volume of the English edition of this work is almost entirely his own interpretation of the notes and material collected by Thayer, that Thayer himself never worked up. In some important particulars it has changed the view that has generally been held of Beethoven's last years; and it is written with as much acumen and penetration and skill in the weighing of evidence as sympathy and reverence.

It may truly be said that this quality of reverence for the great men of music made Krehbiel a purist. He was wroth with any who attempted to tamper with the works of the great masters as they had left them; and this brought him into notable conflict with men who thought that their reputations entitled them to do what they pleased. With this reverence was connected a great love of beauty and a grave dissent from all efforts to make of music something that he thought was not, in some way or other, a manifestation of beauty. Music was to him a pure idealism, and he fought with everything that he thought tended to lower its ideal purity. He had always respect for what he considered sincerity, mastery, and disinterestedness in art and artists and a hatred for the pretentious, the feeble, the bombastic, the insincere, and the incompetent; and especially for self-seekers, who use the art to advance their own interests.

If there was narrowness in some of Krehbiel's views as a critic, it was the outcome of his complete confidence in his own judgment and the validity of his own knowledge and opinions. He brooked, indeed, little opposition. He was apt to lay down the law; as his opponents, and the opponents of criticism in general, like to say, to "pontificate." Pontification is not a good thing in any art, and it perhaps involves a misconception of the function and the limitation of criticism. The critic is not a law-giver; nor does his judicial function extend, like that of the Supreme Court, to the final and definitive interpretation of fixed and unchangeable laws. But Krehbiel had something like a certainty that there were unchangeable laws, not man-made but inherent in the nature of things, in the art of music; that he knew what they were, and that it was his function to lay them down and expound them, as a final jurisdiction, from which he recognized no appeal.

Krehbiel had a native intellectual power and vigor that would have put him among the leaders of any profession that he might have adopted.

Musical Discourse

He chose one that he loved with an enduring passion and that kept him a poor man. His analytical prescience and his extraordinary memory were always serving him; and he put them freely at the service of others. His great knowledge of his special study was always at his command, not only for himself but also for whoever asked him, friend or stranger.

A man of positive opinions, fearless in putting them forth, scorning ulterior influences that have no place in a sincere cultivation of music, he made enemies. He never thought of staying his pen when there was evil to be attacked. But he made friends and admirers innumerable in the half-century of his work. Personal friends cherish the memory of a warm and gracious personality; there have been others all over the country who have been in his debt for the strength and vigor of his writing that brought stimulus and refreshment and opened new horizons; many whom he never saw owe him gratitude for personal kindness and assistance.

THEODORE THOMAS

IT is hard to estimate the debt that the United States owes to Theodore Thomas. It is the debt of a pupil; or it is the debt of a people led out of a wilderness to the prophet who had shown them a sight of the promised land. To him, more than to any other single force, is due the present state of musical culture in the United States. To an amazing persistency in the face of repeated discouragement and piled-up difficulties he joined the fine and catholic taste, and most of all, the willingness to make his propaganda gradually, that were precisely the qualities requisite for his success. He knew that there were many kinds of good music; and that the love and appreciation of the greater kinds were best attained by a gradual uplift through the lesser.

There was, in a way, something of the irony of fate in the fact that Thomas was taken by death just as his ambition and that of his Chicago supporters had been realized, of installing his orchestra in the hall built as the endowment and permanent home of the institution. What he hoped for, his life long, a hope that his friends adduced as the cause of his leaving New York, was a permanent guarantee for the support of his work. This he had never succeeded in obtaining in New York. The offer of it was at least one of the reasons for his taking up in Chicago the work that so long occupied him in the Eastern city.

He had an iron will, an absolute intention of having his own way, and of brooking no interference, a willingness to put up only with the best, an indifference to expense. It was a masterful personality; and he was clearly a man intended by fate for greatness and for the ruling of men. He was a self-made man, and there were those who insisted that some of the defects of his early training were never overcome. He was blessed with an iron constitution and his mode of life made unlimited demands upon it. For years he took an ice-cold bath every morning and went from it to a gymnastic apparatus with which he developed his muscles to such an extent that he could take up almost any of his subordinates and lay him upon the table without an apparent effort.

Thomas came to New York, as he says in his autobiography, in 1845, "when the Metropolitan city was a provincial town of two-story houses and the pigs ran through Broadway and ate the refuse." He had to fall to at once to help support the family and played in a dancing school and in theatrical orchestras — they played better music then than they do now, he assures us,—and made his first acquaintance with Beethoven's "Coriolanus" overture in a performance of Shakespeare's tragedy; for which it is as well suited, probably, as for Collin's tragedy, for which it was written. He gives a diverting account of a trip through the South that he made alone in 1849, as a lad of fourteen:

"I do not remember taking anything with me but my fiddle, my little box of clothing, and some posters which I had printed announcing a concert by 'Master T. T.' I kept a supply of these posters in my trunk, and when I had no money I first obtained permission to use the dining hall of a hotel for a concert, and then I went around on the day before the concert took place and put up my posters with tacks. When the time for the concert arrived I would stand at the door of the hall and take the money, until I concluded that my audience was about gathered, after which I would go to the front of the hall, unpack my violin, and begin the concert."

In one place in Mississippi he affirms that he was ordered by the authorities to leave town, because they believed the devil was in his fiddle! All this speaks as plainly as need be of the energy and self-reliance that characterized Thomas's whole career.

In the next following years he played in New York in orchestras that supported Jenny Lind, Sontag, Mario, Grisi, Bosio, Alboni, and others. It may easily be imagined that the pure and musical quality of their art was of value in forming the taste of an impressionable boy and gave him a valuable preparation for his later task. He himself takes occasion to emphasize the important musical influence of Carl Eckert, the conductor who was brought over with Henrietta Sontag in 1852; and declared that he was "the only really fully equipped and satisfactory conductor who visited this country during that period." The next year Thomas became concert-master under Arditi in the orchestra that supported Lagrange, Mirate, and Badiali — Mirate being, in Thomas's opinion, "the greatest tenor he ever heard in voice, compass, method, and musicianship." In 1853 he had his first experience in a large concert orchestra, under Jullien, the fantastic charlatan, who, nevertheless, did something for good symphonic music, and gave Thomas valuable experience. In 1854 he joined the Philharmonic Society, playing under Theodore Eisfeld, whom he characterizes as "a time-beater," and then under Bergmann. What he says about the latter is interesting as touching an important figure in the earlier

days of musical New York. Some have thought that
Bergmann was Thomas's model in conducting. He
would undeceive them. Eckert was the one who in-
fluenced him and from whom he learned. Bergmann
he considered to be without most of the qualities of
a first-rate conductor; but he possessed "an artistic nature and was in sympathy with the so-called
'Zukunftsmusik'"— the "music of the future." He
lacked the force to make an impression and had no
standard; nor did he study.

One of the most interesting and valuable of
Thomas's early experiences was as a member of the
chamber music organization that he formed with
Dr. William Mason in 1855. Dr. Mason once re-
lated how this came about. On his return from
study with Liszt, he had brought with him Schumann's quintet, then unknown in America, and
Brahms's trio in B. He consulted Bergmann as to
the formation of his ensemble. "I've got the very
man we want," said Bergmann; "he is a young
man named Thomas and he is a violin in my orchestra." The upshot of it was the formation of the
Mason and Bergmann Quartet, including Thomas
as first violin, Joseph Mosenthal as second violin,
and G. Matzka as viola, Mason being the pianist.
Their performance of Brahms's trio, on November

27, 1855, at Dodworth's Hall, was its first performance in public anywhere; and "to the lasting musical distinction of America," as Miss Florence May says in her life of Brahms, inaugurated the public performances of Brahms's chamber compositions. But, as Dr. Mason went on to say in his story, the masterfulness of Thomas made itself apparent at the outset. His interpretations did not agree with Bergmann's, and the result was that at the end of the second season Bergmann dropped out, being succeeded by Bergner. For the decade and more that the organization held together, Dr. Mason declared, Thomas's influence was the dominant one.

The story of Thomas's first appearance as a conductor is told by Dr. Mason as having occurred in 1860. Carl Anschütz was conducting a season of opera in the Academy of Music. On December 7, Anschütz fell ill suddenly — although other accounts have it that the illness was due to one of the financial disagreements of those days. The audience was already seated, and word was sent to Thomas at his home asking him to conduct the evening's performance. He had never conducted an opera before, and the work to be given, " La Juive," was new to him. He got into his evening clothes,

[298]

hurried to the Academy of Music, and conducted
the opera without a mishap. The position of conductor was thereupon given him as a permanency
and he was started upon his real career. In two
years more he decided to devote himself entirely to
orchestral conducting. In 1862 he had been elected
conductor of the Brooklyn Philharmonic; but he
wished a larger and a freer field. He also wished
for better conditions in rehearsal. His account of
the rehearsals of the New York Philharmonic, of
which he was at that time a member and became
afterwards conductor, gives force to his opinion
that they were "not salutary" in their influence
upon the public. Subscribers to the concerts were
at that time admitted to the rehearsals, which was
supposed to be a valuable privilege; but

"The orchestra was often incomplete. If a member had an engagement, he would go to it instead
of to the rehearsal. When one of the wind choir was
thus absent, his place would be filled for the occasion as best it could be. A clarinet or oboe part
would be played on a violin, or a bassoon part on
the 'cello, etc. The conductor therefore could not rehearse as he ought, and the audience talked at pleasure. Under these circumstances justice could not
be done to the standard, much less to the modern

and contemporary works. Such conditions barred all progress."

It was part of Thomas's purpose to put a stop to this sort of thing. He ruled his orchestra with a rod of iron and everybody played his part at rehearsal as he was expected to at the concert. The first concert given by Thomas was in May, 1862, at Irving Hall, and was popular in its character. The orchestra played the overture to "Der Fliegende Holländer" and "the music to the tragedy of Struensee" by Meyerbeer, the latter for the first time in America; Dr. Mason played Liszt's arrangement of Schubert's Fantasie, Op. 15; Bruno Wollenhaupt a movement from Molique's violin concerto; four pianists played Moscheles's quartet for pianoforte, "Les Contrastes"; Mme. de Lussan sang two operatic airs, and a chorus sang a hymn. Thomas's regular "symphony soirées," as he called them, began in December, 1864, with Beethoven's eighth symphony, Lachner's suite in D and the second part of Berlioz's "Roméo et Juliette" symphony, these two for the first time in America. S. B. Mills played Chopin's F minor concerto and Miss Fanny Raymond sang two operatic airs. These concerts lasted till 1878, with a break in the years 1870 and 1871, when he spent all the time travelling. Various departures from his regularly accepted duties as an orchestral conductor, such as his brief period as director of the College of Music in Cincinnati and as conductor of the American Opera Company—a company started with a lavishness that ended in bankruptcy—brought him chiefly conflict and annoyance. So did his efforts to make the musical programme an important part of the Columbian Exposition in Chicago in 1893. He had had a similar unfortunate experience in the Centennial Exposition in Philadelphia in 1876. While there is every reason for music to aspire to a dignified and important place in such expositions, the actual conditions prevailing in them are not favorable to such aspirations and they have seldom succeeded. So Thomas found by disagreeable experience.

Lack of support caused the abandonment of his own symphony concerts in New York after the season of 1887–88. New figures had come upon the scene, notably Dr. Leopold Damrosch and Anton Seidl, with whom there was a good deal of competition. Thomas's position was no longer the unquestioned and exclusive one that it had been in previous years; and he was fretted by the undermining of his supremacy. He continued, however, with great success to conduct the New York Philharmonic Society and the Brooklyn Philharmonic Society till his departure for Chicago in 1891. In that year his friends in Chicago had completed arrangements for an orchestra established upon a permanent basis and called him to be its conductor. This position he held till his death fourteen years later, in 1905.

It was inevitable that a man of such an aggressive personality, such an unyielding will, should make enemies and rouse opposition; and Thomas did both. There have been those who affirm that nothing he ever did was done at any sacrifice to himself; that he spent money lavishly, but always the money that somebody else had supplied, and that one of his talents lay in his ability always to surround himself with men who would put up money for him. Similarly, there have been those who have declared that his reason for leaving New York in 1891 was because he had exhausted this support. Others said it was because he was piqued by sharp criticism of his orchestra, his programmes, his manner of conducting; and because he was hurt by the praise given to other and rival organizations. Many have combated these interpretations, and look upon him as a victim of ingratitude, of a fickleness of public taste that, they point out, has become

Theodore Thomas

more and more fickle in the modern conditions surrounding the work of a conductor. His removal to Chicago was productive of great good to the musical life of that city; the orchestra that he established there has become one of the great ones of this country and its history is one of the most important chapters in the history of music in America. It is in every way a worthy addition to the great work he did in earlier years for the development of the musical life of this country.

Of Thomas's breadth of view and catholicity of taste, too much cannot be said; and the great mass of his programmes that are published in the second volume of his "Autobiography" give ample demonstration of them. That he himself grew through his labors in the field of music was inevitable; yet it will scarcely be accounted as characteristic of him that he should be ready to acknowledge it. A friend once took occasion to remark to him upon the splendid results he had achieved in influencing public taste in his popular concerts—upon his gradual raising of the standard till he was able to rely upon the public's appetite for a symphony. It was put as being his work of instruction. "Oh, don't say that," was his prompt response: "we have grown together." He was one of the first and most ardent admirers

of Wagner. Brahms he early appreciated. As we
have seen, he took part in the first public performance of a chamber composition by the master; and
he did much to introduce his symphonic works to
the knowledge and love of this public. The Philharmonic programmes of his first two seasons, 1877
and 1878, contained the first two symphonies of
Brahms, then new. Tchaikovsky and Dvořák he made
familiar in New York when they were scarcely more
than names in most European capitals. Rubinstein's
symphonic works appeared on his programmes almost as they came out. Richard Strauss's symphony
had its first performance anywhere under Thomas.
Walter Damrosch has left an amusing record in his
autobiographical book, "My Musical Life," of the
competition that went on in the later '70's and '80's
between his father, Leopold Damrosch, and Thomas,
to get first possession of newly published scores from
Europe, and to perform them first in New York. To
go through Thomas's programmes, even down to
his last season, would be to find them full of new
things by men of talent of all schools. The list of
"novelties" that he performed in his last Chicago
season was twice as long as the similar list of any
other orchestra. Nor was Thomas's course in this
regard the outcome of an indiscriminate desire for

novelties, for their novelty only. Not a few such things that he went to trouble and expense to obtain were, after he had examined them, silently put away in the closet and never played, because they were not good enough. He kept abreast of the times in a way that few other conductors have ever cared or dared to do.

Time and again Thomas saw the work he had done apparently brought to naught by the settling down of public indifference or the fickleness of public taste. One after another his enterprises were declared to have failed. He began again on others, and in a new way; and, to a later view, it seems as if none of them had failed, and that what he did was for a permanent foundation, built on a rock. His various series of popular concerts in his early days all saw the line of ignorance and indifference steadily pushed back, and the greater public led and tempted to know and to love good music. The "Thomas concerts" sowed good seed lavishly throughout the country and his efforts have all borne good fruit. Most of them had to be given up, sooner or later; but

'T is not the grapes of Canaan that repay,
But the high faith that fails not by the way.